PRAISE FOR *EXCELLENCE WINS*

Horst Schulze created a culture of service that should be a model for all of us. By committing to the highest standards of professionalism—and creating the right systems to achieve them—he inspired thousands of people to embrace and embody the core ideal of sheer unadulterated excellence. With this profoundly useful book, Schulze now shares his story, and his methods, so that the rest of us can be uplifted and taught by the master himself.

Jim Collins, author of *Good to Great* and coauthor of *Built to Last*

Horst Schulze's influence on my family and our business is undeniable. His approach to customer service revolutionized the hotel industry and set a high bar for all of us. His new book, *Excellence Wins*, weaves Horst's personal story with the practical wisdom he's gleaned from an incredible career of servant leadership. It's a must-read for leaders and anyone passionate about serving people.

Dan Cathy, chairman, president, and CEO of Chick-fil-A

Industry luminaries regard Horst Schulze as the leading hotelier in the world, but his influence extends far beyond the hospitality business. There's a reason for that. He has been *the* thought leader on customer service for decades. We now have the Rosetta Stone of superior customer service—his new book. *Excellence Wins* can only be described as profoundly helpful to any leader who aspires for his or her organization to be the best.

Dr. Tim Irwin, *New York Times* bestselling author and leadership authority

In *Excellence Wins*, Horst Schulze's inspirational story and experienced wisdom gives you the road map to success at the highest levels. This book is a must-read for every manager, executive, and anyone who strives for excellence in their life.

Kay C. James, president of the Heritage Foundation

Horst Schulze is one of the most beloved, creative, and successful hoteliers in the world. His reputation for excellence in all he pursues has generated a global following among stakeholders in his various hotels and other businesses that is legendary and real. People today, regardless of whether they worked with him directly or have learned of his charismatic leadership from others, rightfully honor and revere him as one of the most important and esteemed original thinkers in human development our world has seen.

Richard J. Stephenson, founder and chairman of the board, Cancer Treatment Centers of America®

For an inspiring, practical approach to becoming a preeminent leader in business, nonprofits, government, and academia alike, *Excellence Wins* fills the bill. This engaging memoir depicts a philosophy of leadership that has become the signature trademark of iconic hotelier Horst Schulze, the premier service guru and top visionary thought leader in the hospitality world today. As an academic dean speaking to college students everywhere, I encourage you to read this book and adopt its teachings to spark your own passion for excellence, creating a pathway to tremendous success in your personal and professional lives.

June Henton, dean of the College of Human Sciences, Auburn University

EXCELLENCE WINS

A NO-NONSENSE GUIDE TO BECOMING THE
BEST IN A WORLD OF COMPROMISE

HORST SCHULZE

COFOUNDER OF THE RITZ-CARLTON HOTEL COMPANY

WITH DEAN MERRILL

ZONDERVAN

Excellence Wins
Copyright © 2019 by Horst Schulze

Requests for information should be addressed to:
Zondervan, *3900 Sparks Dr. SE, Grand Rapids, Michigan 49546*

ISBN 978-0-310-35213-6 (audio)

Library of Congress Cataloging-in-Publication Data

Names: Schulze, Horst, 1939- author. | Merrill, Dean, author.
Title: Excellence wins : a no-nonsense guide to becoming the best in a world of
   compromise / Horst Schulze, with Dean Merrill.
Description: Grand Rapids, MI : Zondervan, [2019]
Identifiers: LCCN 2018028392 (print) | LCCN 2018060126 (ebook) | ISBN
   9780310352105 (ebook) | ISBN 9780310352099 (hardcover)
Subjects: LCSH: Customer services. | Customer relations. | Leadership.
Classification: LCC HF5415.5 (ebook) | LCC HF5415.5 .S4445 2019 (print) | DDC
   658.3--dc23
LC record available at https://lccn.loc.gov/2018028392

Published in association with the literary agency of Wolgemuth & Associates, Inc.

Cover design: Curt Diepenhorst
Cover photo: Sandoval Design & Marketing LLC
Interior illustrations: Sandoval Design & Marketing LLC
Interior design: Kait Lamphere

Printed in the United States of America

20 21 22 23 24 25 26 27 28 /LSC/ 15 14 13 12 11 10

*In appreciation to my family
for their patience and support
during the many years
of my heavy travel schedule.*

CONTENTS

PART ONE:
Serving Your Customers

PART TWO:
Engaging Your Employees

PART THREE:
Building True Leadership

FOREWORD

When Horst Schulze asked me to write the foreword for *Excellence Wins*, I was honored. Why? Because for more than forty years, among the many hundreds of top CEOs and company presidents I have worked with around the world, Horst Schulze is easily in my top five.

My observations of Horst when he was president and COO of the Ritz-Carlton Hotel Company gave me a clear image of the impact a leader can have on an organization. Horst has always had a both/and philosophy about results and relationships—and he has put that belief into practice with the people he serves, the customers they serve, and the organization as a whole. Horst and I clearly agree that profit is the applause you get for creating a motivating environment for your people so that they will take care of your customers.

Throughout his career, Horst has modeled his leadership philosophy in three ways that really resonate with me—and you'll read about all three in this book.

1. **Horst has always been a dreamer and a visionary.** When he was a child in Germany, he told his family he wanted to work in a hotel. They tried to redirect him to other careers

every step of the way, but he would not be dissuaded. He was determined to follow his dream. As a young man at the end of a three-year hotel apprenticeship, Horst coined the phrase "Ladies and Gentlemen Serving Ladies and Gentlemen," which became the driving mantra not only for himself but also for everyone who has ever reported to him. I'll never forget visiting Horst at his office at the Ritz-Carlton in Atlanta. I was privileged to witness one of the stand-up meetings he held with staff at the beginning of every week when he was in town. He wanted to make sure people knew where they were heading, give them an opportunity to bring up any concerns they had for the week, and review at least one of the hotel's standards of service with them. In terms of his vision of excellence, Horst has always believed in repetition and reinforcement as the best way to sustain the exemplary service standards taught to each hotel staff member.

2. **Horst has always seen his employees as business partners.** People both inside and outside the Ritz-Carlton Hotel Company couldn't believe it when, many years ago, Horst instituted the policy empowering every employee to spend up to $2,000 to make sure a guest is happy. He trusted his people's judgment—and he loved to collect stories that proved he was right. I particularly like the one about a housekeeper named Mary who flew from Atlanta to Hawaii because a guest had forgotten his laptop computer in his room. He needed it for a big speech he was giving at an international conference in Honolulu the following afternoon. Mary didn't trust that the overnight courier would get the laptop to the

gentleman in time for his speech, so she delivered it herself. Did Mary take advantage of the opportunity to have a quick vacation? No! She flew back to Atlanta on the next flight. What do you think was waiting for her when she arrived? A letter of commendation from Horst and high fives from her colleagues around the hotel.

3. **Horst has always been a classic servant leader.** I'll let you read his own words from chapter 6 of this book:

> Very few people come to work to be negative or to do a lousy job. People come to contribute to a purpose. When we invite them to join us, to take on positions that befit them, their talents can blossom. We haven't just grabbed them off a shelf . . . we have gotten to know them as human beings and carefully matched their unique interests with a set of tasks that energizes them. As a result, they become employees of excellence for a long, long time, which benefits not only them personally but the organization as well.

I'm so glad you picked up this book. You'll love the pearls of wisdom on every page that come directly from Horst Schulze's experience—wonderful stories and lessons to apply in your own organization. By the end, I know you will understand the truth in the title of this book: *Excellence Wins*.

KEN BLANCHARD, cofounder and chief spiritual officer of the Ken Blanchard Companies, coauthor of *The New One Minute Manager*, *Raving Fans*, and *Servant Leadership in Action*

ACKNOWLEDGMENTS

I think it is the norm (as a way to start a book) to write a few words of thank-you to all who impacted my life, work, thinking, and career, which in turn is reflected in this book.

Well, to thank everyone would take half the pages of this book. Surely none of this could have been done without the support of a loving wife—thank you, Sheri! And the love of my children. Thank you, Yvonne, Alexis, Brook, and Ariel. You all sacrificed so very much. You all are very special!

Thank you, all who were impactful on me and my career. Thank you, Karl Zeitler—my first maître d'—Colgate Holmes, Otto Kaiser, and Pat Foley.

Thank you to all who were involved in the early creation of the Ritz-Carlton. It would not have been possible without you! So thank you, Ed Staros, Joe Freni, and Sigi Brauer. Thank you, doormen, waiters, bellmen, housekeepers, chefs, busboys, etc., etc., etc.

I love you all!

FIRST OF ALL . . .

Before we start to explore the main principles of the book, let's talk for just a moment about what to *call* the public we all wish to serve.

If you're in the general business arena, as I am, you will speak most naturally about "customers" or "guests." I'll be doing this throughout the coming chapters.

If you're a consultant, adviser, or counselor, you'll probably call them "clients."

If you work for a government entity, you'll say "citizens" or "taxpayers."

If you're in the nonprofit sector (churches, mission agencies, associations, advocacy groups, and the like), you'll talk about "members," "donors," or "constituents."

If you're an educator, you will refer to "students" (and "parents").

If you're a doctor, nurse, hospital administrator, or other health care professional, your term of choice will be "patients."

But in reality, the people you serve are all the same. They are all people who want us to meet their needs—and we know we must do so if we are to stay viable in today's busy, interconnected world. The label doesn't matter. The inner desires and feelings, the values, and the interests of the person are central.

So as you read, make the applications to your particular environment, seeing what fits your specific challenges.

Let's begin.

A BOY WITH A DREAM

I hadn't even gotten home from school that afternoon before my mother heard about the outrageous thing I had said in class. I was still playing *Fußball* (soccer) with my friends when a nosy neighbor came to report me.

"Do you know what your son said in school today?" she asked breathlessly. "He said that when he grows up, he wants to work in a hotel!"

In our small German village, every self-respecting family wanted their sons to aspire to one of two futures: a technical position (for example, engineering or architecture) in a big city like Munich or Stuttgart, or else winemaking here at home, since the hillsides all around were covered with vineyards. If neither of these came to be, you could at least be a carpenter or a mason.

To talk about hotel work was like saying you wanted to be a street sweeper or a garbage collector.

Where had I, at age eleven, gotten such a crazy idea? Our village didn't even have a hotel—or a proper restaurant, for that matter. To this day, I cannot remember the source of my notion; I must have read about it in a book.

But I would not be dissuaded. My uncle from the city, a respected banker, came to visit once and asked what I had in mind. Would I be going on to *Gymnasium* (high school) in nearby Koblenz? I told him my dream, thinking surely he would understand.

"What? Are you just going to be one of those sloppy guys serving beer in the railroad station?" he scoffed, referring to the small bar in the depot where passengers could get a drink while waiting for the train. He was as embarrassed as the rest of the family.

This standoff went on for three years, until I reached age fourteen—a fork in the road for European students in those days. Either you went on to higher academic study, or else you opted to learn a trade. My parents sat me down one day and said, "All right, Horst, tell us about this."

"I want to work in a hotel. I want to work in the kitchen, in the dining room. I want this to be my work for life."

They looked at each other and knew I was not going to give up. So with a sigh, they decided to help me. They went to some kind of government labor bureau to inquire about what to do next. There they learned of a six-month boarding school for hotel work that was eighty miles from our village. They reluctantly enrolled me and said a tearful good-bye to their son.

Starting at the Bottom Rung

It was an intense course of study, and I was very homesick. But after I finished the program, the school found an apprenticeship for me at a fine hotel and spa in Bad Neuenahr-Ahrweiler (*Bad* in German means a mineral bath or spring, thought to be helpful for relieving arthritis and other ailments). Next to the facility was a clinic whose doctors treated the patients. The hotel was named the Kurhaus ("cure house").

Some wealthy guests didn't visit the Kurhaus for medical reasons; they just came for the concerts in the big garden every afternoon and evening or for the casino.

I still remember the lecture my mother gave me on the train. "Now, son," she sternly declared, "this hotel is for important ladies and gentlemen. We could never stay there." (My father, a World War II veteran, worked for the postal service.) "You must behave yourself accordingly. Take your shower! Wash your socks! Do not do anything out of line!"

We got off the train at last and schlepped my suitcase the ten blocks to the hotel—taking a taxi was out of the question. We met with the hotel's general manager, an educated man who carried the title "doctor," for a brief introduction. He reinforced my mother's warning. "Young man, this place is for important people. They come here from around the world. They are the upper class who truly understand service. Do not allow yourself to become jealous or envious. You are here to serve them." I dutifully nodded my head.

After kissing my mother farewell, I moved into a dormitory room with three other boys. The toilet and shower were located down the corridor. By the next day, I was plunged into the busy life of a busboy. Well, to be precise, the only task I was allowed to do in the beginning was to clean ashtrays. "Be careful," I was told. "Don't disturb the guests while they are eating."

A bit later, I was assigned to wash dishes. The hours were long—from seven in the morning until eleven at night. We set up the dining room before every mealtime—not only the tables, but also the utensils and other supplies the waiters would need. We cleaned the floors. Sometimes, at the end of a tiring day, we had to polish the guests' shoes that had been left out in the hallway. We did everything, it seemed.

Gradually, I was allowed to hand-carry the food orders from the waiters to the kitchen staff and then to bring the food back to the waiters for serving. Then came actually serving the food myself from a side table, dishing up the plates. If meat needed to be carved, however, the maître d' would come over and handle that part.

This was my life for every day of the week except Wednesday, when our young group was bussed to a hotel school in a nearby town. We arrived back late in the afternoon, changed clothes, and immediately went to work in the dining room.

It was hard work, but I never second-guessed my decision. I found encouragement in my mother's letters, which she wrote every day. She would tell me what was going on in the village, what vegetables she was picking from the garden, and then she would always add, "We love you so much. We think about you constantly. We cannot wait for the next time you get to come home for a visit." Sometimes she would even send me grape sugar tablets, which she was convinced would bolster my energy for my work.

Man of Excellence

The maître d', Karl Zeitler, made a huge impression on me. Though in his early seventies, he still had a stately bearing as he would go from table to table, conversing with the guests. At one table he would speak German; at the next, English; at the next, French. His presence filled the room.

In fact, as I watched, it almost seemed as if the guests were proud to have him stop by their table. They looked up to engage him in conversation. This conveyed to me that, while we young workers naturally viewed him as the most important person in the room, the guests apparently thought so too. *What a reversal!* I thought. *It's almost upside down.*

Herr Zeitler was a great teacher for us young people. Before mealtimes, he would talk through the day's menu, explain any new items, and coach us on how to describe them to the guests. The mystique of the industry seemed to dance in his eyes.

In slow times, he would tell us about the great hotels he had worked in during his long career—in London, in Czechoslovakia. He had been an apprentice himself in Berlin many years before. He told us about his friend who had worked on a transatlantic ship. It all sounded so fascinating. When I went home for a weekend visit every three months or so, I had so many stories to tell.

But Herr Zeitler didn't only inspire us; he also held us to high standards. I got in trouble with him a few times. He once caught me helping myself to a quick swig of leftover wine, and he kicked me in the backside! I never did that again.

One time we were serving a banquet at which the entrée was a beef filet and a veal filet, side by side on the plate. As I served a particular guest, he said, "No beef—just the veal." When I returned to the kitchen, I checked to see if anyone was watching me, and then I quickly slipped the beef filet into the back pocket of my trousers, under the formal tail of my jacket.

Unfortunately, the maître d' saw what I had done. He chased after me and dumped hot sauce in my pocket! And he proceeded to give me quite a scolding.

The Essay

One Wednesday near the end of my three-year apprenticeship, we were all assigned to write an essay about how we felt about our work and what we were learning. I didn't know what to say. I sat that evening in my little room pondering.

I decided to write about Herr Zeitler. I told about what an exceptional human being he was. I described his impeccable dress, his elegant mannerisms, his genuine interest in each and every guest. It came to me that he was defining himself as a true gentleman.

Somewhere near the end of my essay, I coined the phrase *Damen und Herren im Dienst zu Damen und Herren*—"Ladies and Gentlemen Serving Ladies and Gentlemen." Like the maître d', we could be ladies and gentlemen as we went about our work. We were not just servants in the shadows of the service industry. We would rise to a higher identity, if we deserved it.

My paper got an A grade (the only A I ever received!). The school's prefect and my teacher even called the other faculty members together for me to read it to them. In that moment, I thought about my uncle and the others who had been embarrassed for me to go into this field. I said to myself, *See, I was right. I can be proud of myself here. I can be respected by others, and I can respect myself. I can be a gentleman.*

A Motto for Life

Close to my eighteenth birthday, I went to work for the winter season in the Bavarian ski resort of Garmisch-Partenkirchen.

Next I went to Bern, Switzerland, to the Bellevue Palace (the official guesthouse of the Swiss government) and also to the Beau-Rivage Palace in Lausanne. Then came the Plaza Athénée in Paris, followed by London's Savoy—all of these were five-star hotels. At one point along the way, I signed on with a Holland America cruise ship, which brought me to New York for the first time. In those days, it took three days to refresh a ship before the next voyage, which meant we had time to explore the city, using our seaman's passports.

While most of my friends jumped into taxis to head for the Empire State Building, Madison Square Garden, or the Statue of Liberty, the number one destination on my list was the famous Waldorf-Astoria. I had dreamed of seeing that grand hotel for a long time. Now I stared up at the big clock in the beautiful lobby. It gave me chills of excitement.

Would I ever get to be the manager of a hotel this splendid? There was no way to tell. But I knew that if the chance ever came, I would seek to make it a place where a staff of ladies and gentlemen served ladies and gentlemen with pride. My dream would be turned into reality, for the benefit of not only the guests but also everyone who would serve them, from the newest maid to the highest supervisor. Together we would rise to excellence.

In this book, I will share how my motto has been put into practice along the way.

PART ONE

SERVING YOUR CUSTOMERS

CHAPTER ONE

GETTING INSIDE YOUR CUSTOMER'S HEAD

Sometimes what the customer wants may seem completely self-evident. If you're selling hot dogs at the ballpark, obviously the fans want hot dogs—at the lowest possible price. If you're running a school, parents want their kids to be educated—while paying the lowest possible taxes and fees. If you're operating a hospital, patients want to get well and go home as soon as they can—while you do all the insurance paperwork for them.

Yes, what the customer wants seems like common knowledge. It's easy to come up with a quick answer. But that answer barely scratches the surface of what the public is actually looking for. If you don't dig deeper, you will miss important signals. You may, in fact, even wind up responding *against* what your market is craving.

Shortcuts That Mislead

Some of our assumptions can hinder understanding and even be outright dangerous. Have you ever caught yourself saying any of these things?

- "I already know . . ."
- "My wife [husband] said the other day . . ."
- "I was talking to my neighbor [friend or workout partner at the gym or whomever], and they said . . ."

All of these statements are nothing more than a "survey of one." They tell you the thinking of a single human being—one out of the multiplied thousands you hope to reach. Any statistician will tell you that's too small a sampling to be reliable.

The practice of bringing together focus groups—eight or ten people sitting around a conference table giving their opinions—can be a bit more helpful, although not unless rigorous follow-up analysis takes place. For one thing, the setting is terribly artificial; a conference table is not where people live their daily lives. If the subjects are being paid $50 or $75 to be there for an hour or two, that can skew their remarks even more. And again, the sampling is extremely small.

Widening the Pool

So then, how can you as an organization leader get input from a wide enough pool of individuals for that information to be meaningful?

One way to do this without spending a fortune is to pay attention to ongoing surveys of customer/member satisfaction. All too many leaders are in the mode of "tell, tell, tell" ("promote, promote, promote" or "preach, preach, preach") without giving the public a chance to answer back. What do they really think of your product or service? What do they like? What is irritating them? What do they think you could be doing better? And perhaps the best yardstick of all—would they recommend you to any of their friends?

This feedback can be gathered in various ways: comment cards, follow-up phone interviews, or online questionnaires.

Granted, the purists would say these are not scientifically random samplings, since people can choose whether or not to cooperate. And of course, the loudmouth complainers will always jump at the chance. That is why you must be careful to watch for *trends* over a period of time rather than simply reacting to individual gripes (again, a "survey of one").

If you find the load of raw data overwhelming, you may want to hire an outside company to do the analysis for you. They can sift and sort, categorize and summarize, so that you come away with usable information. Yes, it will cost a little money, but you can gain a great treasure of insight. Or you can go to larger firms that specialize in organizing and researching customer service measurements from start to finish. I happen to think that J.D. Power is the best, having used them repeatedly both here and overseas. But there are others worth considering as well. They can analyze *trends of dissatisfaction* but also *trends of demands*—for example, "If you would add X or Y to your services, the public would be much happier."

Again, I repeat, you don't need to just react to a few ax-grinders. Instead, you can listen to the market to gain valuable information.

This process is a lot more important than simply comparing ourselves to our competitors. For a while, a big buzzword in business was *benchmarking*—in other words, seeing how you stand compared to the rest of your particular industry or market segment. But that's not the point. And it's not necessarily helpful. As I bluntly told one fast-food executive who asked me how I thought his company was doing, "You're the best of a bad lot!"

A better form of benchmarking is to measure how you're

doing compared to how you were doing a year ago or three years ago. Are you making headway? Do you have a higher percentage of people who are pleased with your service?

Getting to the Bottom

Sometimes the feedback you receive will seem cloudy, so that you're not quite sure what it signifies. Customers may not always be able to articulate what they're truly feeling. I remember one set of focus groups in which people kept saying about their hotel stays, "I want to feel at home."

It was a sweet, warm sentiment. But what did it mean? What did it really tell me? Obviously, I couldn't furnish and decorate every room to look like each incoming guest's personal home.

I hired another firm to listen carefully to the session recordings and try to discern what was really being said. They came back to me with this interpretation: *They want to feel something from their subconscious memory—what they used to feel in their mother's home.*

And what was that? Their childhood home had been a place where everything was done for them. Every need was taken care of. Somehow the lightbulbs got replaced and the grass got cut without them giving a thought as to how those chores happened. They didn't have to worry about a thing.

If anything did seem wrong, they immediately went to their mother. "Mom! Mom! Something is really bad—I don't have any socks in my drawer!"

And what did their mother do? She said, "Come here, sweetheart," and wrapped them in her loving arms. She knew exactly what to do to solve the problem. What she did *not* say was, "I'll call the manager about that"!

But this happens in business every day.

I learned that deep down inside, hotel guests want to feel assured that everything is under control, and that any problem will be resolved right away. They don't want to wait three hours. They want to unload their feelings on the closest person they see. They want somebody—anybody—to care for them. If this happens, they will feel respected and even honored.

Based on this, I announced a new policy: *Every employee, from the general manager down to the newest busboy, is empowered to spend up to $2,000 to make sure the guest is happy.*

Suppose a guest comes to the restaurant and hears the hostess say in a cheery voice, "Good morning, sir! How was your night?"

"Not the greatest," the guest may reply with a frown. "The toilet kept running, and I couldn't get it to shut off."

The hostess should immediately answer, "I'm so sorry about that! Please forgive me. I will take care of this right away. And we're going to buy your breakfast now to make it up to you." Then as soon she has seated the guest, she will jump on the phone and insist that the hotel maintenance person fix the toilet before the guest gets back to his room.

When I announced this policy, my peers nearly fainted. The owners of the hotel thought about suing me. I answered, "Look, the average business traveler will spend well over $100,000 on lodging during their lifetime. I'm more than willing to risk $2,000 to keep them coming back to our brand of hotels."

This was not driven by any desire to throw money away, obviously. It was driven by the knowledge of what the customer really wants. I made a decision that we would move heaven and earth to serve that particular expectation.

Real knowledge of the customer is absolutely essential. Without it, you cannot serve your market in a way that is superior to the competition.

Three Universals

You may be saying, "But I'm not in the hotel business. My arena is different."

No matter what field you're in, I can guarantee (after processing thousands of customer comments) that the people you serve want three main things.

First, they want a product or service or other output with *no defects*. Let's say you're selling them a bottle of water. They want the water to be absolutely pure—no little "floaties" swimming around. They also want the bottle to be leak-proof. They want to know they can trust this purchase 100 percent.

When I talk about defects, I'm thinking not just of *physical* defects—say, a sticky door or a noisy toilet. I'm also including *process* or *system* defects—the kind of thing that leads customers to say, "Hey, I never got my receipt," or "Where's my suitcase? I have to be dressed for a banquet in three hours!"

My collaborator on this book, Dean Merrill, recently flew from his Colorado home to Dallas for a family funeral. The death had taken the man's children by surprise because he had seemed to be feeling all right, even at age eighty-six. But one day, his daughter-in-law showed up at his home with her father-in-law's usual morning coffee and doughnut, only to find he had collapsed on the carpet.

In the midst of the family's shock and grief, they took an EMT's recommendation of a funeral home less than a half mile down the boulevard. Early arrangements went smoothly. But when family and friends showed up for the 10 a.m. Monday morning funeral, it was a different story.

First, the information placard telling people how to get to the chapel had a completely different man's face and name on it. "Oh, sorry about that," said the person working in the office. "That was left over from a viewing last night; we'll switch it out right away." *Defect no. 1.*

The service began with a welcome, the reading of Psalm 23, and a prayer. But something else was distracting the guests. *What's that noise outside the window?* everyone wondered. They figured out it was the *rrrrr* of a riding lawnmower. The irritating sound went on for at least twenty minutes. Did someone really need to be cutting the grass at that particular time? Couldn't the job have waited until the funeral had ended? *Defect no. 2.*

Later in the service, the program called for playing a beloved recording of the man's deceased wife, who had a wonderful soprano voice, singing the Andraé Crouch song "To God Be the Glory." This was designed to bring back wonderful memories of the man for all the mourners. And the song was to be accompanied by a slide show of family pictures from over the decades— the happy couple, Christmas gatherings with the grandkids, memorable vacations, and the like. One of the sons had spent hours gathering these photos, sequencing them, and uploading them to the funeral home website. The audio track ran fine, but for some unknown reason, the pictures wouldn't show on the big screen. The software kept crashing. *Defect no. 3.*

After the service, burial was slated for the family plot outside a small town some ninety miles away in East Texas, where the man had grown up. Given the distance, there would be no formal procession; instead, all attendees were given clear directions for driving there on their own. The route wasn't complicated: just go east on Interstate 20 to a certain exit, turn right, and then travel on a state highway for ten miles until reaching the cemetery.

The various family members all arrived around 12:30. The cemetery staff had done their job. The square tent was erected; the folding chairs were in place; and three workers stood respectfully at a distance, leaning on their shovels.

But no hearse. Fifteen minutes went by, then twenty. Eyes kept scanning the horizon. The one son who had made the arrangements pulled out his cell phone to call the funeral home, only to be told, "He's on his way."

A full half hour passed, then forty minutes. Little great-grandchildren grew restless, wanting to play in the dirt. A baby had to have a diaper change in one of the vans. The son called again. This time the report was even worse: "We can't seem to get in touch with the driver. We're not sure where he is."

When almost an hour of waiting had passed, the exasperated son said, "Well, everyone, listen up. Let's all just go to the restaurant where I've made reservations for our family meal. We can come back later for the graveside ceremony."

The hungry, hot, tired group started walking toward their vehicles, thoroughly frustrated, when the hearse bearing the casket rolled slowly into the cemetery. The driver's only explanation: "I got lost." *Defect no. 4*—the biggest of all, and on a day when people's emotions were already raw.

An alert business stays one step ahead to prevent this kind

THE PEOPLE YOU SERVE
WANT THREE MAIN THINGS

FIRST
THEY WANT A PRODUCT OR SERVICE OR OTHER OUTPUT WITH NO DEFECTS

SECOND
THEY WANT TIMELINESS

FINALLY
THEY WANT THE PERSON WITH WHOM THEY'RE DEALING TO BE NICE TO THEM

of thing. Or if something goes awry once, they immediately call a staff meeting to make sure it never happens again.

Second, the people we serve want *timeliness*. They don't want to have to stand or sit around waiting for you. If they're eating in a restaurant and their meal comes out absolutely perfect and tasty (no defects), but it took forty-five minutes to be served, they're going to be unhappy, regardless of how delicious the meal is. If someone calls your customer service line and is put on hold for ten minutes, it won't matter if the agent is totally smart and competent to solve their issue. The customer is going to be so ticked off that they will hardly notice.

Finally, they want the person with whom they're dealing to *be nice to them*. They want to sense a caring attitude. In fact, this third desire is greater than the first two combined. It can atone for other shortfalls. I have actually heard restaurant customers say, "I had a problem with the food—but the waiter did such a great job, and the chef even came out to my table and apologized. So it all turned out fine."

I was in Chicago once to speak to the executive team of a certain bank. The afternoon before, I decided to check out their operation. I walked into this massive institution in the downtown Loop area and gazed at the impressive marble pillars. The whole ambience exuded wealth. Twenty-four tellers were at their stations serving customers.

I took my place in line and waited to be called. When I finally got to the head of the line, what did I hear?

"*Next!*" a young woman's voice rang out.

I approached her station and said, "I'd like to change this fifty-dollar bill."

Without a smile or any word, she took my money and did

what I asked. In rapid fire, she counted out my change aloud: "Ten, twenty, thirty, forty, forty-five, fifty. *NEXT!*" I took my handful of bills and scooted away.

Had the bank teller delivered a product with *no defects*? Yes. She gave me the correct amount of money. And all the bills were genuine; none were counterfeit.

Had she done this in a timely manner? Yes. Our whole exchange took less than sixty seconds.

Had she shown any hint of relating to me as a human being or caring about me? *No.*

I told this story to the bank executives the next morning. Then I asked, "What industry are you in? Surely the service industry! You don't manufacture any money; the US Mint does that part. All you do is handle other people's money, right?" They begrudgingly nodded their heads.

I made some more remarks and then said, "When I entered your bank yesterday, I assure you I did not feel like I was being served."

Let's say you're in the medical field. When people come to a doctor's office, they, of course, want to get rid of their pain. But that is not the whole picture by any means. Healing resides in more than just the pill bottles on the shelf. Patients want *to be heard* by the doctor, the nurse, even the check-in assistant at the front desk. They want someone to listen to them with a caring heart. Yes, their recitation of symptoms may be lengthy, as well as confusing—but it's their reality. If the medical professionals don't engage with their humanity, the healing process can be inhibited.

When you walk into a church, you naturally expect the preaching to be biblical (no defects). You expect the service to start and end at the stated hours (timeliness). But along the way, does anyone notice you—anyone, that is, besides the official "greeters" who have been told to do so? Does a pastor or elder look you in the eye and smile or shake your hand? Are you made to feel that you matter in some small way to this large and busy institution?

Granted, not everyone wants to be affirmed in the same way. Some people go for enthusiastic hugs, while others feel encroached upon by physical contact. But at least a smile and a warm "good morning" would let you know you're valued.

Worshipers come to connect with God, of course. But they'd also like to connect with a fellow human being or two. As the wise and beloved nineteenth-century British preacher Joseph Parker is reported to have once said, "There is a broken heart in every pew."

And Furthermore . . .

I've noted that two more customer desires have arisen in recent years. No matter what your standard product may be, people these days seem to be more and more interested in individualization and personalization.

Individualization. People want to be able to tweak a product to their own likes—which makes it challenging for any of us who aspire to serve large numbers of people. But customers don't think about that. They just know they don't want to be locked into a fixed menu. The Subway sandwich chain has risen to the top of its market by letting folks decide how much lettuce, black olives, grated cheese, and jalapeños go on their particular sandwich, and they're allowed to watch the assembly process every step of the way. The car industry has known for a long time that the more options and gadgets it offers, the more new cars it sells.

At the Ritz-Carlton Laguna Niguel in Dana Point, California, I started noticing complaints at the facility about our noon checkout time—especially on Sundays. People had come to enjoy a long weekend of sleeping late and then going to the beach, and they felt pressured by the clock.

We moved our checkout time to 3 p.m., and the complaints disappeared. Of course, this meant we had to adjust our staffing, bringing in more housekeepers for the later afternoon hours to turn over the rooms more quickly. But that was a small price to pay to create a positive experience for our guests.

Later on, we asked ourselves, "Do we really have to make people obey rigid checkout deadlines at all?" We studied our clientele and realized that the majority of guests voluntarily clear out early enough in the morning to allow us to clean their rooms for the next guest. Why apply and enforce an unnecessary rule? Consequently, we did away with checkout requirements altogether.

In another hotel, one of our housekeepers noticed while emptying the wastebasket in a certain room that the guest had picked out the nuts from the chocolate chip cookies he had gotten from the club lounge tray. What did she do? Just ignore this information? No, she mentioned to the chef that this guest apparently didn't like nuts. The next evening when the guest returned to his room, he found waiting for him on the bedside table a tray of chocolate chip cookies without nuts.

She had taken individualization to a whole new level.

In certain situations, focusing on the individual can make a huge difference. Southwest Airlines got major accolades in 2015 for the way it handled a situation involving a customer named Peggy Uhle. Peggy was sitting in her seat ready to take off from Chicago's Midway Airport and head for Columbus, Ohio, when all of a sudden, a flight attendant approached her and said, "I'm sorry, but you need to leave this flight. Come with me, please."

Peggy thought she might have boarded the wrong plane. But then the gate agent directed her to a nearby service desk, where she was told to call her husband right away. There she learned that their son, who was in Denver, had suffered a severe injury to his head and was in a coma!

Obviously, Peggy no longer wanted to fly east; she wanted to get to her son as soon as possible. The Southwest Airlines team had already figured this out and rebooked her on the next flight to Denver. They retrieved her luggage from the Columbus-bound plane, retagged it, offered her a private waiting area, and even packed her a lunch for the Denver flight—which they allowed her to board ahead of everyone else.

"The care that I was shown was second to none," the distraught mother said later. "We've always liked Southwest Airlines, and now we can't say enough good things about them."

She was at her son's hospital bedside within hours, thanks to a caring airline. Her son's condition has gradually improved since then.[1]

Personalization. No sound on earth is as sweet to a person's ears as their own name. They don't want to be "Account Number W49836Q7." They want to be called by name; it's a recognition of their worth. In the hotel business, we train doormen to check the luggage tags on the suitcases they're unloading from the taxi so that as soon as the guest finishes paying the driver and steps out, the doorman can say, "Welcome, Mr. Johnson!"

Of course, if the name is too hard to pronounce, it's better not to try and then end up getting it wrong. If you're sending a birthday card to a customer who was born in July, make sure your systems are in order so that you don't mail it in October. That will do more harm than good.

Shifting Sands

Even when you think you've mastered what the customer wants, beware of changing tastes. When I started in the hotel business, our studies showed that at the busiest check-in time (early evening), guests were willing to wait in line for the next front-desk agent for up to four minutes. We took steps to have staff people reach out to them after just two minutes, offering perhaps a soft drink.

But people today are less patient. They get annoyed after just twenty seconds! We've had to ramp up our service personnel as a result.

It is quite possible to lag behind the ever-shifting culture or even to get too far ahead of it. I learned this the hard way in the first Ritz-Carlton hotel when we implemented the VingCard electronic lock system to open room doors. We were proud to be on the cutting edge of technology at that time. But guests said, "What is this—some silly little piece of plastic? You're supposed to be a luxury hotel—you can't afford to give me a real room key?" We quickly changed the locks back to metal keys.

Three years later, the plastic alternative had become accepted.

People were used to them, and they now viewed traditional keys as downright dangerous. "What if I lose this key and somebody finds it? They'll come barging into my room at two in the morning!" We had to change the lock system *again*.

The same thing happened when we first introduced voice mail. I thought this was the way to go. But people said, "You don't want to deliver a handwritten message to my room anymore? What kind of a cheap joint is this, anyway?" So we did both methods for a while—paper messages plus the electronic system. It didn't take long, of course, before voice mail became widespread in offices and homes, solving the problem and simplifying our system.

All of this illustrates that customers' preferences keep changing. If you think you know them well today, you will still need to keep learning next year and the next and the next. Organizations and their leaders have to keep adjusting.

Double or Triple Audiences

In more than a few situations, the leader is in the tough position of having to understand and please multiple populations. For example, the Red Cross has to serve the people who've just been flooded out as well as the donors who are footing the bill. The school principal has to please not only the parents of students but also the educational bigwigs in the state capital and in Washington, DC. The plant manager has to get along not only with the wholesalers (who will merchandise the finished products) but also with the labor unions. Every publicly held retailer has to not only please the customer in the mall but also make

Wall Street happy. Hopefully the contented customer buys more, which makes the investors happy too. But not always.

Leaders often find themselves attempting a juggling act. They cannot afford to ignore their core constituents, obviously, or there will be no tomorrow for anyone. They must find ways to prove to the external players that this is good business all around. We'll talk more about this dynamic in the coming chapters.

But for now, let the main point be clear: understanding what means most to the public we serve is essential, even if it is not always easy.

CHAPTER TWO

CUSTOMER SERVICE IS *EVERYBODY'S* JOB

The instant I say "customer service," business leaders nod their heads in agreement. "Oh yes, customer service is very important. We need to provide good customer service."

But I fully believe the term is not well understood. If you ask even the leaders of "service companies" such as banks or hotels to define customer service, they mumble generalities. I have repeatedly asked these leaders, "How do you teach service? What is your process?" only to find that they have few specific answers.

It reminds me of the famous quip often attributed to Mark Twain, "Everybody talks about the weather, but nobody does anything about it." Well, while we may not be able to do anything about the weather, in the case of customer service, we *can* do something about it.

If you think customer service is merely a desk in the back corner of the store (or a call center cubicle in faraway India, where a polite young man or woman with a thick accent reads from a script while trying to solve your problem), you have sorely shortchanged the concept. Too many people think customer service starts after a complaint has been voiced. Somebody has gotten upset about something, and the point of customer service is to try to calm them down.

But that's far from the truth. Customer service starts the instant you make contact with an individual.

First Step

Customer service starts at the front door or with the first ring of the phone. The first step of service is **offering a great welcome**. You show immediately that you are glad the person has chosen to come your way—even if they haven't bought anything so far and you're not sure if they even want to.

I have taught my hotel staff that this welcome needs to happen as soon as the person gets *within ten feet* of them. Immediately they must say, with genuine sincerity, "Good morning!" or "Good afternoon!" If this doesn't happen, the potential customer can start to feel self-conscious. *Am I in the right place? Do I belong here or not?* But if the welcome is warm and immediate, the individual makes a subconscious decision that's positive. They're willing to explore further.

Notice that I said "within ten feet." I didn't say "fifty feet." If someone enters a store and an employee stocking shelves four aisles away hollers out, "Welcome to Joe's Bargain House!" it does no good. The customer can tell that the greeting wasn't sincere. The type of welcome I am advocating must be honest and personal.

After analyzing hundreds of thousands of comment cards over the years (with the help of the esteemed J.D. Power research firm), I learned that if a customer's first four contacts with our hotel go well (for example, the phone reservation clerk, the doorman, the bellman, and the front desk), there will be virtually no complaints thereafter. But if something goes amiss in the beginning, the complaints will sprout quickly: "The check-in was too slow." "The room wasn't clean enough." "The food was too cold."

And on and on it goes. Some of these complaints may not even be true. But the mood was set at the start.

Second Step

The second step is **complying with the customer's wishes**. The focus here is not on your agenda, but theirs. Yes, you want to make a sale. But what is most important is what is on *their* mind.

That is why you say, "How may I help you? I'm happy to do so." And then you listen—really listen to see what is front-of-mind for them. They may not be very articulate about it. They may stumble around trying to explain what they want. You have to play detective sometimes. In auto repair shops, service managers (notice the language) especially must do this. Someone drives in and says, "Well, my car is making kind of a funny noise. I'm not sure what's going on." The customer is worried about it enough to drive in. He doesn't know if it's something silly, like the hood not latching tightly enough, or if the whole transmission is about to fall out. Regardless, the service manager has to figure out the problem with the car and address the customer's concern.

Third Step

We've had the great welcome and have complied with the customer's wishes. Now comes the final part of customer service, which is **saying good-bye**. It's always important to say, "Thank you for coming in today," or "Thank you for allowing us to serve you." NBC's José Díaz-Balart has a good closer for his weekend broadcasts: "Thank you for the privilege of your time." In this he recognizes that, even though he's a nationally famous and well-paid journalist, viewers did not *have* to watch his show. They did so voluntarily, and he is truly grateful for their time.

A sincere good-bye makes people feel positive about a return visit. Whatever skepticism they may have harbored about the organization is being replaced by trust. Inside their head, they're saying, *They sound like they like me. Maybe I'll go back again.*

Not Just for Frontliners

Customer service isn't just for those who face the public. It also extends to people inside an organization who deal with each other. Really, it's all connected.

In any food operation, the cook working in the back of the kitchen serves the waiter. You may have thought that the fellow in the tall white hat was the prima donna of the kitchen, barking out orders and telling everybody else what to do. Not at all. The food that the cook prepares has to please the guests, or else the waiter is going to get an earful. Chefs must realize that the waiters are their internal customers, so to speak. They are the conduits to the final customer, who, after all, is the person paying everyone's salary. Of course, on the other hand, the chef can be the nicest, most conscientious person in the world, turning out great food, but if the waiter is rude to the guest, the chain breaks down.

Every employee in every department needs to figure out who their internal customer is. If they don't know or are confused by

CUSTOMER SERVICE ISN'T JUST FOR THOSE WHO **FACE** THE **PUBLIC**

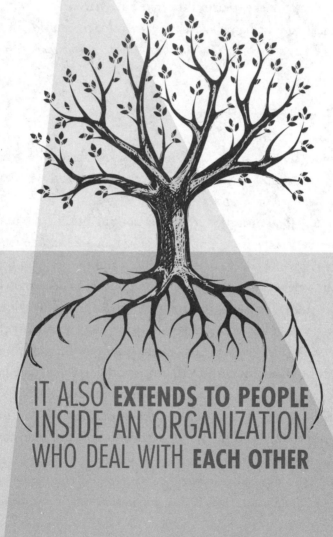

IT ALSO **EXTENDS TO PEOPLE** INSIDE AN ORGANIZATION WHO DEAL WITH **EACH OTHER**

the question, management must help them clarify, so they can then ask this individual, "How can I make things better for you? What can I do that will help you better serve *your* customer?" In this way, the work will flow better.

Everyone, from the newest dishwasher on up, should know that their primary responsibility is *to help keep the customer*. If the customer in the restaurant says to the waiter, "Uh, this spoon has spots on it," that tracks back to the dishwasher. Customer service has been compromised in that moment.

Stop and Help

Even internal staff members can have random contact with customers. The maid who cleans the rooms and makes the beds when guests are out may still pass some of them in the hall. The guests need to be greeted warmly. If they have a question, they deserve a friendly answer—or at least quick access to someone who can provide an answer.

The great Stephen Covey, renowned for his international bestseller *The 7 Habits of Highly Effective People*, was sitting in one of my hotel lobbies one day while a maintenance man worked high on a ladder overhead. A woman approached the door with both arms laden down with her purse, a couple of packages, and luggage. The maintenance man quickly scrambled down the rungs of the ladder to hold open the door for her.

Covey couldn't resist following up to say to the man afterward, "Excuse me—that was a very nice thing you did for that woman."

"Yes, well, that's how we've all been trained," he replied.

He proceeded to pull out of his back pocket the small placard containing our "Credo" with its twenty-four Service Standards. "See here?" he said. "Number four says, 'We assist each other, stepping out of our primary duties to effectively provide service to our guests.'"

Covey was amazed. "Does every employee have one of these folders?" he asked.

"Oh yes," the maintenance man replied. "We go over one of these points at the start of every shift, so that we cover them all in a month's time."[1]

It wasn't long after that incident when I received a call from Stephen Covey. "Next time I'm in Atlanta, I want to get together with you," he said. It was the beginning of a long and warm friendship that lasted right up to his death in 2012.

Years ago, a business consultant wrote that after going into dozens of troubled companies to try to help them, there were two warning signals he heard most often from the staff. The first warning signal was the overuse of the pronoun *they*. This telegraphed a rupture between departments or between upper and lower echelons. "Well, *they* won't let us do such and such," or "*They* messed up," or "*They* just don't get it." The second statement revealing a warning signal is, "That's not my job." In other words, *I have my own little box of expertise, and don't anybody dare to ask me to step outside of it!*

This is why I'm not a big fan of desks with signs reading "Customer Service." It sends a silent message to the rest of the employees that they don't have to mess with such problems or serve customers because "Customer Service" will take care of it. No!

Instead, the desired goal in every organization should be that, through everything that's done (from saying hello to mopping the floor), the guest is persuaded to come back. This is a far greater goal than just checking off certain tasks. It is making a valuable impression.

Benedict's Rule

Serving others is not some novelty or leadership fad of the current century. You can trace it all the way back to at least the Middle Ages. You may have heard of Saint Benedict (AD 480–547), who wrote an extensive manual on how monasteries were to treat those who were passing through. Here are some excerpts:

> All guests who arrive should be received as if they were Christ . . .
>
> As soon as a guest is announced, then let the Superior or one of the monks meet him with all charity . . .
>
> The greeting itself, however, ought to show complete humility toward guests who are arriving or departing: by a bowing of the head or by a complete prostration on the ground, as if it was Christ who was being received.
>
> After the guests have been received . . . let the Superior or someone appointed by him, sit with them . . .
>
> Let the Abbot give the guests water for their hands; and let both Abbot and monks wash the feet of all guests.[2]

Obviously in the modern hospitality industry, we don't quite go to these lengths! But you get the general point. We should ask ourselves, How do we stand in comparison to Benedict's monasteries?

Benedict went on to write about job flexibility among the monks in charge of the kitchen:

> They should be given all the help that they require, so that they may serve without murmuring, and on the other hand, when they have less to occupy them, let them do whatever work is assigned to them.
>
> And not only in their case but a similar arrangement should apply to all the jobs across the monastery, so that when help is needed it can be supplied, and again when the workers are unoccupied, they do whatever they are required to do.[3]

Service always implies caring. You and I may not have the same religious orientation as Benedict and his monks, but we can have the same charity in our hearts.

To make customer service a reality, not just a label, we have to hire the right kind of people and orient them thoroughly at the start, and then we have to repeat our values again and again. Every last employee contributes to creating loyalty among customers.

If we settle for lesser goals—meeting the budget, for example, or safeguarding our jobs in a tough economy—we will miss the most important work.

Attending to Details

Many of the smallest things we do have an impact on customers. They listen to how we talk, for instance. I hired high school drop-outs from the inner city to come work for the Ritz-Carlton—and do their work elegantly and excellently! How did I accomplish that, you ask?

I instructed my new hires that when they greeted a guest, they were not to say, "Hi!" or "Whassup?" Instead they needed to say, "Good morning, sir!" or "Good morning, ma'am!" And when a guest asked for something, they were not to say, "Okay" or "Cool" or "Got it." They needed to say, "Certainly—my pleasure. I'm happy to help you."

They were not to call our guests "guys" or "folks." They needed to refer to them as "sir" or "ma'am" or "ladies" or "gentlemen." Why this style? Because we know that guests want to feel honored, even important. "Hi, guys" doesn't accomplish that.

I have lived and headquartered in Atlanta since 1983 and have enjoyed getting to know the leaders of another strong business here—the Chick-fil-A fast-food company. Several times they have invited me to consult with them, and on one such day a few years ago, I was telling this detail about training our employees to speak in a certain way to our guests. I then qualified my remarks by adding, "Now, of course, in your business, I suppose this language doesn't quite fit your market segment. You may want to be more casual."

The group began to brainstorm the kinds of wordings that might be suitable. Sitting silently in the back of the room was S. Truett Cathy, the brilliant founder of the company. Someone had piped up that in his opinion it would be fine for a Chick-fil-A worker to answer a customer request with "Okay, I can do that."

And then . . . the Voice at the Back rose up. "I like 'My pleasure.'" Oh!

I responded, "Well, yes, we use that at Ritz-Carlton, but I'm not saying you have to follow suit. Let's work through what you want to be used in your stores." The discussion resumed.

After a while, the Voice at the Back rose up a second time. "I like 'My pleasure.'"

And that ended the debate!

When an organization builds a reputation for quality service, it creates a unique reputation. If the person out front consistently greets customers with genuine warmth, shows respect, makes sure everything is right, makes the person feel good, and thanks them for the privilege of serving them, the customer will assume the maid, the cook, the bookkeeper, the custodian, and everyone else will be just as pleasant. And if the day comes when any of those employees go out looking for a different job, if they say, "I've worked the past x number of years for such and such a company," they will likely get hired faster due to that organization's prevailing reputation.

Rooting Out Problems

Not everything runs smoothly in all workplaces—that much we know. When there's a problem, the important thing is to track down the cause of each and every customer service deficiency and then remedy it.

Achieving this can be harder than you might think. I got a lesson in this when I opened the very first Ritz-Carlton here in the Buckhead section of Atlanta back in the mid-1980s. We had proclaimed a promise of providing room service within thirty minutes of ordering, and I found that we weren't delivering very well on our pledge. Slow room service in the morning was, in fact, our number one complaint.

So, not knowing as much then as I do now, I hauled the

room service manager into my office and said, "Take care of this. I don't want to be getting these complaints anymore. Make it happen!"

Naturally, he said, "Yes, Mr. Schulze, I will fix the problem."

But the complaints kept coming. Guests would call in the morning to order their breakfasts and say, "Please get it here quickly, because I have to leave soon for a meeting." And then when it didn't happen, they would be upset, grabbing just a cup of coffee on their way out the door. Plus, we'd then have to throw the meal away after the waiter had run up and down the elevator in vain—and received no tip for the effort.

As we opened more Ritz-Carltons in the coming couple of years, my responsibilities widened. But I kept noticing that the Buckhead hotel's complaints for slow room service weren't going down. The numbers were as troubling as always.

By this time, I had studied the Malcolm Baldrige criteria, which emphasize the need to find the root cause of any defect in order to eliminate it permanently.[4] This is a vital part of *continuous improvement* in any organization. So I brought together in one room the staff from across departments—the order taker, the cook, the busboy, the waiter—and said, "I want you all as a group to find the cause of this. Do a study, and send a report twice a week to your general manager on how you're coming along."

They began tracking the steps of a room service order and found:

- The order was phoned in and written down accurately—no problem.
- The waiter read the order and set up the tray (silverware, napkin, and so forth) for delivery—no problem.

- The cook received the order and prepared the food promptly—no problem.
- The waiter put the tray on his shoulder and headed to the service elevator and—bang! He would have to wait up to fifteen minutes there on the first floor as the elevator went up and down the twenty-two floors in the hotel.

Why was this happening?

The group began to hone in on the issue here. The staff knew that the morning breakfast time was naturally very busy for the service elevator. All the housekeeping staff were going up and down, getting themselves and their supplies to the various floors.

The team called in the building engineer. "What's the matter with your elevator?" they asked. "Why is it so slow? You need to join our team and help figure this out."

The building engineer agreed, even though he assured them there was no mechanical problem. Just to underline his point, he called in the Otis elevator people to do an inspection. They confirmed that nothing was wrong with the equipment.

For the next step, the team decided to dispatch one of their members to ride the service elevator in the morning and see what was really going on. After all, it shouldn't take more than two minutes to go all the way up and back down. If there were passenger pickups along the way, maybe it would require four minutes instead of two. But not fifteen.

The "scout" put a small stool in the elevator and took a seat to watch.

The elevator started on the ground floor, went up to the fourth floor, and stopped for a houseman. (In the hotel business, the houseman is the person who supplies the maids on the various floors with linens, soap, shampoo, and so forth.) He got on board and punched the button for the fifth floor, and when the door opened again, he pulled out a wood block to keep it open while he went out to the supply room and returned with an armful of linens. Then on the sixth floor, he proceeded to block the door again while he went out to deliver the linens before coming on board again. This process kept repeating itself, floor after floor.

No wonder the food trays from the kitchen weren't getting to their destinations!

The team now insisted on cross-examining the houseman. "Why is this happening?"

"Because we're short on linens," the man calmly replied. "We only have two sets of linens per bed—one is on the bed and the other is in the laundry. A hotel really needs a third set so it can be in transit. But as it is, we're constantly stealing from each other."

This brought the laundry manager into the meeting—an old-timer who had been at his job from day one. "Why do people need to keep stealing from one floor to the next?" the group wanted to know.

"Because we have only two sets per bed."

"And why is that?"

"Well," the man replied, "before we opened this hotel, there were budget problems. Mr. Schulze needed to save money, so he cut out one set of linens!"

The root cause of slow room service had finally been uncovered. It was my fault after all! And I had been giving grief to several managers unfairly. I promptly authorized the purchase of another set of linens—and the room service complaints immediately went down by more than 70 percent.

But how many guests had we lost because of this? How much time had been wasted running up and down? How many waiters had been frustrated because they hadn't gotten tips? How much food had been scraped into the disposal?

Sometimes a customer service problem—or any defect, for that matter—is rooted as much as five steps away from where it shows itself. One solitary person at a counter somewhere can't solve it alone. It needs the best thinking of everyone connected to the process, because they are fully committed to giving the customer every reason to keep coming back—again and again.

Each time you get to the bottom of a defect in this way, you improve your customer service while simultaneously lowering your cost over the long haul. It's a win-win all around.

CHAPTER THREE

FOUR SUPREME OBJECTIVES

Serving the public successfully is not always simple. Customers (clients, members, constituents) can indeed be grouchy and demanding. Some of them are a royal pain in the neck. It is understandable to get frustrated at times with trying to keep them happy.

But if you let this become your default assumption—that people aren't going to be happy no matter what you do—you're not going to give customer service your best effort. And that is going to hurt you in the long run.

After analyzing thousands upon thousands of comment cards and surveys over the years, I can tell you that 2 percent of customers simply cannot be pleased. They're clearly irrational. They want things you can't afford. Or they want things that will irritate the other 98 percent. I call this small population "the jerk factor."

But even these people do not give us an excuse to stop being ladies and gentlemen. That is who we are and must continue to be, whether others appreciate it or not. We must not be distracted from the four supreme objectives of any organization that wants to succeed:

1. Keep the customer.
2. Get new customers.
3. Encourage the customers to spend as much as possible!—but without sabotaging Objective Number One.
4. In all of the above, keep working toward more and more efficiency.

Whatever your line of endeavor—manufacturing, retail, finance, education, or ministry—this is your assignment. You must never lose sight of these things, no matter how noisy the world around you becomes, no matter how busy you get. You must keep on trying.

I've been told that in the world of fund-raising, many non-profits assume they're going to lose 30 percent of their donors every year. They've accepted this as a rule of thumb—they'll have to find a batch of new donors every year simply to keep pace with the year before.

Granted, a few of those donors will have died. But what about those who just got bored with your appeal for funds and wandered off? Don't you want to know why they walked away? Aren't you interested in learning what you could have done to reenergize them to support your mission?

In fact, I'm told there's a whole ancillary stream of the direct-mail business in which organizations buy and sell lists of "lapsed donors." These are the names and addresses of people who used to give to one cause but have stopped (who knows why), and now the roster of their information can be rented to another cause for x dollars per thousand. The new organization will try to get donations from these people, since the old organization was no longer effective. This is assumed to be normal practice, even though getting a new donor or customer is always more expensive than keeping an old one.

If an entire organization from top to bottom is committed to keeping the customer, trying as hard as possible to understand them and meet their expectations, the results will show in a marvelous way.

Extreme Cases

You may be saying to yourself about now, *But, Horst, some people truly are impossible. You just can't hope to please them.*

Well, if what the customer wants is illegal, then, yes, you must call the authorities. Pleasing the customer is out of the question in that case! Short of that exception, however, there are a number of creative ways to proceed if we simply give it some thought. Once in a great while, we in the hotel business have a guest who is so obnoxious that we're tempted to give up. I made a policy across the entire chain of fifty-some Ritz-Carlton hotels worldwide that the only person who could decide to evict a guest was me. I would not delegate that decision.

One day, my manager in Atlanta called to say, "Horst, we have a guest who's been here ten nights already. Every morning he comes to my office complaining about multiple things. Whatever we try to do for him is never right. And on top of that, he's staying up on the club level—where he has pinched a couple of women! Naturally, they're very upset. Can I please get rid of him?"

We didn't have enough hard evidence to call the cops and file a charge of battery against this man. We hadn't actually seen the outrage ourselves and didn't have security video. But this was serious. We weren't going to just wave this off.

So I replied to my manager, "Okay, here's what you do. One, go double-lock his door while he's away so he can't get back into his room. Two, make a reservation for him at another first-class hotel here in the city. Three, get a limousine lined up and waiting for him. When he comes storming into your office again, say, 'Mr. Jones, for ten days you've been complaining about every-thing. We are here to try to please every guest. So now I'm going to try another way to please you! We're going to move you to another fine hotel. I've already made the reservation; the limo is waiting for you. We truly want you to be happy.'"

The manager followed my orders. And of course, the guy was on the phone to me within minutes, absolutely furious.

"Yes, I know," I interrupted. "I told the manager what to do in this situation. This is all my doing."

"I'm going to sue you!" he screeched.

"Mr. Jones," I calmly replied, "if you sue me, just understand that the ladies you pinched will be sitting there in the courtroom that day."

Silence.

Here's the second half of the story. Six months later, I got a call from our manager in Naples, Florida. "Horst, I have a guy here who comes every morning to my office complaining," he told me. "Not only that, but he pinched some ladies up on the club-level floor."

"Oh, you must have a Mr. Jones in your hotel!" I said with a frown.

"How did you know?"

I then proceeded to give him the same instructions I had given to my manager here in Atlanta.

The Naples manager told me later that as soon as he started into his speech, "Mr. Jones, we are here to please you . . ." the fellow shook his head and said, "Oh no, not again."

No Excuses

However, let's get back to the customers we *are* able to serve. We *can* satisfy more than 98 percent of the public if we put our minds to it. It's simply a matter of attitude.

It's also a matter of not settling for excuses. Over the years, I've heard most of them, like:

- "Well, you know, people are just getting more and more cranky these days."
- "It's a problem with our market segment." Sometimes this gets downright racist or ethnically charged, as in "We're getting too many Asians" or "We have a lot of Russian guests, and they're a bunch of underworld types."
- "There's construction on the street in front of us—a lot of noisy machinery. We can't do anything about that."
- "We've had terrible weather here. A blizzard came through, and nobody was traveling"—an excuse I've heard more than once from hotel managers.

Of course, to some managers, these are not excuses. Instead, they're "explanations." The words sound plausible and make managers feel as if they've answered the question and thus solved the problem. The trouble is, there is nothing beautiful in an "explanation." Beauty lies rather in *innovation*—figuring out how to overcome the challenges and press on to success, to customer pleasure, to achievement.

That is, in my view, the difference between a *leader* and a *manager*. A leader keeps pushing forward to the four supreme objectives: How can we (1) keep the customer, (2) find more customers, (3) maximize their "spend," and (4) become more efficient? In contrast, a manager puts more time into thinking up excuses for not achieving these things.

Sadly, the world has more managers than leaders.

Going the Extra Mile

When everyone in an organization is aligned with these overarching objectives, wonderful things begin to happen. At our hotel on the beach in Cancun, Mexico, a newlywed couple arrived all set to enjoy the honeymoon of their dreams. But on the very first afternoon, tragedy struck. The new husband lost his wedding ring in the sand.

The couple was devastated, of course. The beach attendant got busy helping them look for the ring. He even called in extra staff to get down on their hands and knees, combing through the sand. Nothing showed up. The new bride became hysterical. The rest of that day was very sad.

But was there a creative option that had not yet been tried?

As darkness fell, the staff members didn't just go home with the words "too bad" on their lips. They had been immersed so deeply in the company's all-important objectives, especially the first one: *Keep the customer! Keep the customer!* Four of them asked themselves what else they could do to please these distraught newlyweds.

On their own, they decided to use some of their $2,000 empowerment (I described this in a previous chapter) to go into town and buy four metal detectors. Then they began sweeping the beach area more systematically than they had before.

The next morning when the newlywed couple came down to their breakfast table, there was the wedding ring, waiting for them.

You can imagine the whoops of joy. They wrote glowing letters to the staff, the general manager, and even the executives

AN ORGANIZATION
CAN'T PLEASE
EVERY
HUMAN BEING
EVERY TIME
BUT
IT NEVER
HURTS TO TRY

of Ritz-Carlton, which is how I heard about what had happened. News media picked up the story. It generated a tremendous amount of good publicity for us.

I thought later that if the four employees had asked their boss for permission, he probably would have authorized the purchase of just one metal detector, not four. But the four didn't bother asking. They knew they were empowered to go the extra mile to convince these guests that this was the best hotel chain in the world. And they made the right choice.

An organization can't please every human being every time. But it never hurts to try.

CHAPTER FOUR

THE FINE ART OF HANDLING COMPLAINTS

Have you ever noticed that if you voice a problem or frustration to someone in an organization, a dead stare seems to come across their face? Their tone—if they say anything at all—goes flat. They wait in utter neutrality for you to finish venting your emotions. The sooner they can escape from this conversation, the better.

It's as if they've been schooled by the auto insurance industry, which tells its clients that, in the aftermath of a fender bender, "Be polite, but **don't tell anyone the accident was your fault**, even if you think it was." (That's a direct quote—boldface type and all—from the website of one of the largest insurers, which I shall kindly refrain from naming here.)

Many business leaders seem to think that stonewalling is the best option in sticky moments. They fail to realize that in well over 90 percent of the cases, the customers just want to get rid of their frustration. They often don't want anything as tangible as compensation. They just want to be heard. They simply long to hear the words, "I'm so sorry about that."

The Mouse That Grew into a Monster

Years ago, I heard a business professor from Florida International University tell a story about having breakfast in a coffee shop with a friend. The waiter brought them two mugs of coffee.

After the professor had drunk about half a cup, he discovered a dead mouse at the bottom of the mug!

Immediately, he called for the manager. "There's a dead mouse in this coffee!" he complained.

"No, that's impossible," the manager insisted. "That can't be true." An argument ensued. The manager wouldn't yield to the facts.

The professor ended up suing the restaurant. He went on to tell this story again and again to business audiences all over the country where he was invited to speak, remarking, "If the guy had simply apologized, I might have asked for a free breakfast, but I would never have sued. Instead, he chose to hang tough with me. And he made a bad situation far worse."

An opposite example is seen in what happened with JetBlue Airways in February 2007, when an ice storm hit the Northeast and forced the airline to cancel a thousand flights. Some passengers already on board at John F. Kennedy International Airport were kept in their seats for up to five hours. Soon the entire JetBlue network was a scrambled mess, with pilots waiting in terminals where incoming planes had not arrived, and planes in other cities sitting empty without their flight crews. It took almost a week to recover.

Travelers were incensed, of course. "I'll never fly this [bleep] airline again!" they swore to one another. Industry watchers began to wonder if JetBlue could recover from this major blow to their reputation.

CEO David Neeleman promptly responded with a sincere apology. He told every inconvenienced flyer how sorry he was that their lives had been so disrupted. He even apologized to every employee for the frustration and embarrassment they were experiencing as they dealt with irate customers. He and his

73

staff contacted every media outlet they could. He posted a video apology on the company website.

The whole catastrophe, Neeleman said, might end up costing the company as much as $30 million, but he was committed to regaining the trust of both the flying public and the JetBlue workforce. Changes were made. Neeleman and the board concluded that he, a visionary, should become chairman, while they promoted to CEO a man who was more operations-focused. As a result, JetBlue did not collapse; it still flies today as the sixth-largest airline in the American skies.

Do you see what a little "humble pie" can do?

Tactics to Employ

I believe this method of problem solving is so strategic that I instituted a mandatory two-hour class in problem resolution for all Ritz-Carlton employees. At the end, they even got a certificate to prove they had completed the training. Here are some of the key points we covered together.

1. *Never try to laugh it off or crack a joke, no matter how ridiculous the complainer sounds to you.* Guard even your facial expression. This is dead serious to the person in front of you.
2. *If you get a complaint, own it.* Immediately say, "I'm so sorry." It doesn't matter whether you personally *caused* the problem or not. In that moment, you are the face of the organization, and you speak on its behalf.
3. *Don't say "they" or "them"; instead, say "I."* It does no good

to say, "Hmmm, it looks like *they* messed up." That just frustrates the already agitated person. Instead, take ownership of the mistake or misunderstanding.

4. *Ask for forgiveness.* Go ahead and spit out the words "please forgive me." Notice, you say "me," not "us." Take the sins onto your own shoulders. This goes a very long way in calming the emotions. After all, what is the complainer going to say—"No, I refuse to forgive you"? Are they going to punch you in the jaw? Hardly.

5. *Don't appeal to the policy manual,* as in "Well, our guidelines say that . . ." The upset person couldn't care less what policy 14, section 8, paragraph 3 says.

6. *Don't try to parade your expertise,* as in, "Well, the reason this happened is because the system is set up to recognize certain signals and blah blah blah . . ." The person doesn't care what you know or how your system is designed; they want to know whether you *feel* their pain or not. They just want somebody to hear their angst and validate it. Here's an example from the field of education. Imagine a mother coming to her child's school and saying, "Mrs. Schmidt was really unfair to my Kristen yesterday. She was downright rude. It just wasn't right!" The principal or other administrator must resist the urge to trot out their academic credentials, their long track record of pedagogical management, or their assurance that the teacher in question is very qualified and has always handled student challenges appropriately. That will simply telegraph a message of "we're the professionals here, and we know how to run a school; you're just a mom." She's actually a mama bear rising to the defense of her cub. She may not

have a graduate degree in elementary education, but she has claws and teeth! She can make things very messy for all concerned if the issue is not handled sensitively.

7. Finally, *don't assume that the complainer wants something* (for example, money). Most of the time, they just want to be heard. They want to get rid of the bad feeling inside. They want their viewpoint to be respected. Once that happens, their blood pressure will come way down.

Actually an Opportunity

Believe it or not, a customer or client frustration can become an opportunity to create new loyalty. What is loyalty? Simply a feeling of trust. Every relationship in life starts out with *dis*trust: *I don't know you, and so I don't know if you're going to take advantage of me.* If things move along smoothly for a while, they may get to a state of neutrality: *I guess this person or this company is halfway decent. At least they haven't stabbed me in the back yet.*

Now what if a problem arises at this point? What if there's a lack of service, a misunderstanding, a snafu? And what if the company is quick to own the pain, to apologize, to make things right again as best they can?

The customer goes away thinking, *They really heard me. They took care of my issue. They made amends. I trust those folks.* Such is the accelerating power of the sincere apology and follow-through. The relationship doesn't just revert to its previous state; it winds up better than it was before the problem arose. A new loyalty has been cultivated.

This loyalty, however, is not cast in stone. If the same problem pops up again next month or next season, the customer will understandably wonder if the previous exchange was genuine. *Maybe I shouldn't completely trust this organization after all,* they may think. The dial slips back to "neutral," and trust has to be won all over again.

Each and every difficulty is an opportunity to advance the trust quotient or to squander it.

Reputation Is Fragile

I went to buy a suit and two extra pairs of pants at one of the most famous department stores in America, one with a high reputation for customer service. I picked out the styles and colors I wanted. The tailor took all the measurements and assured me the work would be done.

When I returned to pick up my purchase, I tried everything on. The suit fit fine. On the extra pants, the cuffs fell at my shoe-tops, just as they should. But the fit was too loose in the hips. I knew this because the week before, I had measured the width of the pants in the dressing room, and now I measured them again. It was clear that nothing had been taken in.

I said to the sales associate, "Wait a minute. These pants were supposed to be taken in, and they weren't. The length is fine, but the hip measurement is the same as before."

All he said was, "Okay, let's call the tailor." A new measurement was taken, which produced the same specifications.

"All right, we'll get it taken care of," the salesman assured me. "That will be $80 for additional tailoring. Come back next Wednesday."

"What?" I said. "You must be out of your mind to charge me again! I want to talk to the manager." Did they think I was stupid, or what?

The manager came, listened to my story, and gave a perfunctory apology. She agreed to waive the second charge. But nobody bothered to explain why the work hadn't been done the first time.

I got the product I wanted in the end, but only after a lot of unnecessary back and forth. But you can be assured that I will not be shopping again at that department store, no matter how good their customer service reputation is said to be. They could easily have kept my business with a genuine response, but they didn't.

Handling Threats

Sometimes an apology is not enough to calm down an aggrieved customer. You may try your best to identify with their passions and even compensate for their losses. But they still threaten to take you to court.

Take food poisoning, for example. A customer may say, "I had shrimp at your place last night, and it made me deathly ill! I was up all night. I'm going to sue you!" The fact that your staff may have served sixty orders of shrimp that evening and nobody else got sick cuts no ice with this individual.

You can apologize and say you're very sorry for their discomfort, but when they say their lawyer is going to come after you, the language must change. You reply, "Well, in that case, you and I shouldn't be talking. You need to talk to my lawyers. Their name and office phone number is _____."

This approach alone is sometimes enough to get them to back down. But if a formal complaint letter arrives from this person's lawyer, you will, of course, hand it to your lawyer. You're out of the game at this point. Legal counsel will take over and try to arrange the least damaging resolution. Often the complaint withers away under the glare of deposition. Negotiation and out-of-court settlements will reduce the hurt to your bottom line. Such is the nature of business life in the modern economy.

But most of the time, people who feel they've been offended just want to be heard. They want somebody to listen to them and say, "I'm truly sorry." They want their emotions to be recognized, not brushed aside. An on-the-spot apology, with perhaps even a follow-up handwritten note in the mail, can make wonderful amends. And then life can roll on.

I'll never forget walking into the lobby of the Buckhead Ritz-Carlton here in Atlanta early one morning and being accosted by a guest who recognized me. "Do you realize what just happened?" he practically yelled out. "I gave my valet claim check to your doorman to get my car up from the garage—and he let somebody else jump in and drive away with it!" The entire lobby stopped to listen to this loud outburst.

The valet had apparently gotten distracted and hadn't stayed with the car until the proper owner came out. Now we had a mess on our hands.

Instantly I replied, "I am so embarrassed. Please forgive me! We will call the police right away. And we will give you another car to drive so you don't miss your appointments"—which was easy to arrange, since one of the car companies had a rental desk right there in our lobby.

Within minutes, he had calmed down and was on his way.

By nightfall, the police had found his vehicle and returned it. The guest called me back the next day to thank me for how the problem had been sorted out. What could have been a public relations nightmare turned out positive in the end.

Complaints don't have to become complications. With quick, alert, sensitive handling, they can be resolved and even result in good outcomes for the organization.

CHAPTER FIVE

THREE KINDS OF CUSTOMERS (AND THREE WAYS TO LOSE THEM)

Business and organizational leaders often proudly say, "We have a database of 200,000 customers that we can maximize" or "We now have 3,000 members" or "We're in regular contact with 15,000 constituents." Some claims even run into the millions.

When a business goes up for sale or a merger takes place, its names and addresses are considered an important asset, sometimes valued even higher than its real estate or inventory. There's just one problem, and it's a big one: Those people in Pittsburgh and Paducah and Provo don't consider themselves to be the property of the business! They can drop away at any time. And, in fact, they do.

The minute we start thinking and acting as if we own the customer, we are nurturing a dangerous fantasy.

Three Kinds of Customers

Anyone who has ever done business with us comes in one of three varieties.

Dissatisfied customers. These are the people who feel they got a bad deal. They paid too much for an inferior product. Or their credit card was mishandled. Or the agent was unfriendly. In one way or another, the transaction left a bad taste in their mouth. Forever afterward, these people become terrorists against your organization! They tell their friends how poorly they were treated. They go on social media and rant. They post negative reviews online. Wherever they go, they sow bad seeds about your brand.

Satisfied customers. These are the people who feel that things were "okay." They got what they paid for. Nothing went amiss. Of course, if one of your competitors comes along and offers a better price the next time, they'll readily switch. If the other company will give them a tote bag, a piece of jewelry, or even a fuzzy teddy bear, they'll go for it. They feel no particular allegiance to you.

Loyal customers. These are the people who have actually come to like you (in more than just a Facebook "Like" sort of way). Based on their experience, they trust you to do the right thing. They tell others you're a good organization. They'll stick with you, even if somebody else offers them a discount. They consider themselves to be part of your tribe.

They don't come right out and say, "I trust this company." It's a feeling in their subconscious. When they want the kind of product or service you offer, they automatically turn your way. But as I said in the previous chapter, loyalty is dependent on *continuing performance*. Though a customer has been convinced to stick with you, he or she can easily be "unconvinced" by one or two bad experiences. Customers aren't really yours unless you keep reestablishing and reconfirming that they should keep trusting you, as you consistently deliver what they're expecting.

How to Lose "Your" Customers

When a company loses the trust of loyal customers, it usually does so in one of three ways. The first two are subtle, while the third is dramatic.

LOYALTY
IS DEPENDENT ON
CONTINUING PERFORMANCE

THE MINUTE WE START THINKING
AND ACTING AS IF WE OWN
THE CUSTOMER

WE ARE NURTURING
A DANGEROUS FANTASY

1. You Start to Cut Back on the Promise of Your Brand

Every brand—whether high-end or low-end—is a form of promise to the public: *If you buy this, you're going to get such and such, and you'll be pleased by it.* It doesn't matter whether you're Mercedes or McDonald's. Customers bring certain expectations to the transaction.

When budgets get tight and the business isn't making as much money as last year or last quarter, the temptation arises to take things away from the customer and hope they won't notice. In my field of upscale hotels, a manager will say, "Well, we don't have to keep buying fresh flowers for the lobby, do we? It's just a cost we can cut. That piano over there with the guy who comes and plays in the evenings—we can do without that, I'm sure. The soap in the rooms? Let's make those bars a little smaller. And the towels don't have to be so soft, do they?"

The crazy thing is, this manager will often be rewarded for cutting costs! He may even get the Manager of the Year award. There will be a black-tie dinner at which his smiling face is projected on the big screen, and everyone will clap as he comes onstage to receive a plaque and a fancy trip to the South Pacific. *Bravo, bravo!* Why? Because he trimmed expenses. Meanwhile, his customers are beginning to think less of his establishment. Their expectations are no longer being met. His brand is being steadily diminished.

Corporations are infamous for announcing a round of what they euphemistically call "reengineering" or "rightsizing." What this often means is, "Okay, everybody, cut staff costs by 10 percent." And so there will be a bunch of layoffs in which valuable expertise and knowledge get pushed out the door.

But before long, customers start complaining. New people have to be hired. The head count goes back up—and then the new folks don't know half of what the old employees did and have to learn the business anew.

Don't get me wrong. I'm all in favor of efficiency. We don't need to carry dead weight on the payroll. But efficiency is something very different from mindless cost cutting.

If we truly believe in Objective Number One—*Keep the customer!*—maybe the criteria for Manager of the Year should be *customer retention* instead of cost reduction. What percentage of customers are saying they want to come back? What percentage of customers are saying they'd recommend us to their friends? What percentage of customers are checking the top boxes (9 or 10 out of 10) on their satisfaction surveys? These are the measurements that matter and should be applauded.

2. You Start to Get Careless

It's very easy to stop looking at things through the customer's eyes, not paying attention to seeing what they see. You let yourself become so familiar with the day-to-day operation that you don't notice little slippages.

Let's say a passenger gets on an airplane, and when she lowers the drop-down tray in front of her, there's a coffee stain on it. *No big deal*, you think. But in the passenger's mind, she's thinking, *Hmmm, I wonder what else isn't quite up to par on this airplane. I wonder if the engines have been maintained recently. What about the doors—will they really stay shut at thirty thousand feet? Am I going to be safe on this flight?*

Not long ago, I dropped by a tire store to get an estimate on new tires for my car. Three women were stationed behind the counter. Not one of them looked up to say hello. The mat in front of the counter was dirty. Yes, I knew that out in the shop area, changing tires is a dirty job, but did they have to track the same dirt into the reception area? Off to one side sat a pot of coffee and some paper cups on a table. The smell of burned coffee wafted across the room. No thanks!

I went up to the women and said, "I'd like to get an estimate on a set of tires, please." They got a mechanic to come out and check my car's tire size and write up a quote. The price was acceptable. But I didn't give them my business. Six months later, I bought a set of tires from a different dealer who ran a clean operation and treated me like a human being they truly wanted to serve.

You see, the first store made the mistake of thinking they're just in the tire business. No, they're not. They don't actually make any tires themselves; Pirelli, Michelin, and Firestone do that. The only value the dealer adds is *installing* the tires they acquired from a wholesaler.

In a grocery store, customers notice how fast the checkout line moves. If they're waiting in line, they have time to look down and see whether the checkout aisle is clean. I dare say this means as much to the average shopper as whether they saved five cents on a can of beans. It affects whether or not they want to come back to that store next week.

3. You Start to Become Arrogant

If a customer picks up a hint that we think we're better or smarter than they are, they will run in the other direction. A friend was telling me about his shopping experience in one of the big-name electronics stores. He needed a new router for his home network but wasn't sure which one to buy or how many extra features he needed.

"The salesperson I flagged down seemed to be about nineteen or twenty years old," my friend said, "a total geek who spoke in computerese and was clearly bored with having to educate this ignorant old fogy. The truth is, I do know my way around the internet; I use a computer every day in my business, and I'm not a novice at technology. But I obviously don't know as much as the young guy who eats, breathes, and sleeps this stuff. And his attitude showed it."

When I first came to America as a young man, I worked as a waiter in a French restaurant in San Francisco. All the other waiters, it seemed, were French; I was the only German. They would talk to each other condescendingly about the customers who didn't even know how to "properly handle a knife and fork." The manners of Paris were the right way to do things, and these uncultured Americans obviously didn't get it.

I could sense the arrogance in how they approached each table of guests. It went against everything I had been taught years before by my first maître d' when I was still a teenager. Weren't these guests paying the bill that supported all our salaries? Shouldn't we be treating them with respect and honor? Didn't we want them to come back and spend more money with us on other nights?

The food in this restaurant, I have to tell you, was excellent. The chef and his team definitely knew what they were doing. The furnishings were elegant. Even so, within a year, that restaurant went out of business. People had picked up the hostile vibe in the air, and they stopped coming. Elegance without warmth is arrogance.

More recently, we were all shocked to learn that one of this nation's foremost banks had been caught opening more than two million phony credit card and loan accounts that customers didn't ask for so that the bank could meet sales quotas and charge extra fees. It's unbelievable! How dare they?

"The problem," said a business professor at the prestigious

Wharton School of the University of Pennsylvania, "is either outright fraud from the highest levels or a broad indictment of the Wells Fargo governance system . . . The idea [i.e., excuse] that Wells management initially advanced—that this was just a few bad apples—doesn't add up anymore." One of his colleagues on the same faculty added, "Before the crisis, Wells was the most valuable bank in the world. Since then, its price-to-book value ratio has fallen by 31%. Moreover, Wells has been losing market share to other banks not tainted by this scandal."[1]

This is a classic example of arrogantly and greedily optimizing the "spend" (Objective Number Three) at the expense of Objective Number One ("keep the customer"). In the end, everybody loses.

The Limitations of a Loyalty Club

In closing, one more tactic needs our scrutiny. It is common these days for businesses to elicit customer loyalty by inviting them to join clubs. The airlines started this several decades ago, offering "miles" for travel that would turn into free flights in the future. Since then, everyone from food outlets to hardware stores has joined the parade.

There's nothing particularly wrong with this, as long as we don't deceive ourselves into thinking these club members are now "ours." No, they're not—even if they've agreed to pay $59 or more a year to join. That layout of money in November is long forgotten when they're making a purchase decision the next April. If they are not in love with our product or service, they're not going to put up with it another time just to get points.

Besides, the novelty has long since worn off. By now, "the average American household belongs to 28 loyalty schemes," says *The Economist*. "More than half of these accounts go unused . . . They are so common that they end up generating little fidelity."[2] Plus, do you really want to haul around twenty-eight different plastic cards in your wallet or purse?

I was in a management meeting of a company that was noticing slight losses in customer retention. Their reservations for the future were slipping. "What are we going to do about this?" the boss wanted to know.

One answer came quickly: "Let's tweak our point system." In other words, they thought if they'd give the customer a few more points for using their facility, they could get the numbers back up.

Nobody seemed to think about improving their core product. After a while, I went up to the flip chart and drew a picture of a cup. "This water in the cup is your current business coming in from customers," I said. But then I added some drops that leaked out of the bottom of the cup. "What are these drops? Customer dissatisfaction. Apparently, there are things they don't like, and so they're moving away from you. Maybe we ought to talk about this, do you think?"

If the product itself doesn't hold the customer, nothing else will. If the guest experience doesn't convince them to keep coming back, we must ask ourselves why not.

Loyalty is cemented not by extra points, gimmicks, or goodies. It is rather confirmed by fulfilling the customer's expectations every time they make contact with us. The difference maker is consistently delivering what the customer wants in the first place and assumes they'll be getting from us. Only then will they keep choosing to give us the privilege of their business.

PART TWO

ENGAGING *your* EMPLOYEES

CHAPTER SIX

MORE THAN A PAIR OF HANDS

magine you're running a paint store, a lawn care service, or a tourist information bureau. Now think about your workplace at midnight on a Thursday night. There sits the copy machine, silent and dark except for the little green power light. Every chair around the room is vacant. Outside the window, the company vehicles sit motionless in the moonlight, locked up tight. You bought (or leased) each of these items to fill a need in your company.

What's missing?

Your staff, obviously. They certainly aren't spending the night at work, patiently waiting for your next command. They've gone home to their families and friends, carrying on with the rest of their active lives outside your business. They have kids to take care of, spouses to talk to, groceries to purchase, TV shows to catch up on, phone calls and text messages to return, and a hundred other things to accomplish. Plus, at this hour, they're in need of sleep! Not until after the sun rises on Friday morning will their attention turn back to you.

About now you're probably saying to yourself, *Well, duh—of course.* But how many times do business leaders slip into thinking of human beings as little more than what might be called "function fillers"—bodies hired to do a certain task—and nothing more? They serve no purpose greater than the chair or the copy machine in that they're useful tactically, but that's all.

Henry Ford was a brilliant engineer who deserves credit for perfecting, among other things, the modern auto assembly line.

Whereas other cars were being built a piece at a time by one—or maybe a few—craftsman, Ford envisioned a long line of workers attaching their assigned parts as the chassis slowly moved along. A stroke of genius, to be sure.

But it had a dehumanizing effect on the workers. Ford apparently didn't think much about this though. It is said that he once complained about his personnel department, "Why is it that every time I ask for a pair of hands, they always come with a brain attached?"[1] He also didn't fully appreciate the individuality of customers, it seems. That's why he is quoted as having said, "Any customer can have a car painted any colour that he wants so long as it is black."[2]

When we identify an operational function and then go looking for a warm body to fill that function, we are being short-sighted. We're treating *people* as just another category of *things*. I believe this is not only bad practice, but even immoral. It ignores the God-given talent and worth of the human being. It depersonalizes them, reducing them to the level of office supplies.

Beyond Taylorism

Whether we realize it or not, we still have one foot in what academics call Taylorism, named after the industrial engineer Frederick W. Taylor (1856–1915), who said that in order to mass-produce efficiently, an operation needs some people (the few) who *think* and other people (the many) who *do*.[3] The smart people should set up the operation and tell the rest what to do to make the widgets come off the line smoothly and quickly. Whether the workers get to appreciate the finished product, or even see it, is beside the point. The goal, said Taylor, is to keep the operation humming.

Many bosses today no longer quote Taylor, but they carry out his philosophy when they say things such as, "We have to be aligned." What does that actually mean? Too often it means, "I'm leading the parade, and you need to stay *in line* behind me. Don't get *out of line*."

Far better to say to a potential employee, "Do you want to know what our company is about? *We are bent on becoming the best in our category.* That's our objective. In fact, that's what we dream about. We look down the road three years, and we can see ourselves being ranked number one in this city. To reach this goal, here's our belief system. This is who we are. Is this purpose anything close to what you'd like to join? Do you want to help us get there? It's going to take a lot of hard work from all of us. But it's going to be great!"

If the person says yes, we can go on to explain, "Here's what this would mean for you personally: respect, recognition, opportunity, the chance to build your reputation in this industry, and yes, money as well. All kinds of good things are in store."

If, on the other hand, the applicant realizes that deep down inside they wouldn't really enjoy this line of work, would rather be in a different field, or would prefer to reside in a different part of the country, then it would be silly to hire them, no matter how strong their résumé.

The challenge is to cast a vision and then invite other living, breathing human beings to join you in pursuing that vision. This is probably the most important strategy a leader can undertake. It is so much grander than just sifting through a stack of applications and picking out a few that stand out to plug into open slots. If we're just hiring to keep day-to-day functions running, whether it's making sausages or checking in hotel guests, that is sick leadership.

We need to go back and again read Adam Smith, the Scottish economist best remembered for his book *The Wealth of Nations*. Yet he considered his earlier book *The Theory of Moral Sentiments* (1759) to be superior. One of his brilliant, if unconventional, insights in that book is that human beings cannot relate to *orders and directions*. They relate instead to *motives and objectives*.

I believe Smith was exactly on the mark there. Employees respond enthusiastically to motives and objectives. They simply endure—put up with—orders and directions. Yet what do we leaders dish out most these days, nearly three centuries later?

Maybe back in the Great Depression, with unemployment running at 25 percent, our grandfathers knew they had to shut up and accept whatever slot was open because they needed work so badly. But we're not in the 1930s anymore. Men and women have a greater sense now of what they want in a job. The trouble is, some bosses are still mired in Great Depression thinking. They learned it from managers of that era.

I remember a certain hotel manager in Hong Kong who listened as I talked with his room service staff. I was saying things like, "You are empowered here. I want you to say what is wrong so we can improve. What can we do better in this hotel? Talk to us about these things!"

At the end of the meeting, the manager said, "Excuse me, Mr. Schulze, I am quitting."

I was surprised. "Why?" I asked. "What is the problem?"

"You're allowing the employees to speak up," he answered

EMPLOYEES
RESPOND
ENTHUSIASTICALLY
TO
MOTIVES
AND
OBJECTIVES

THEY SIMPLY
ENDURE
PUT UP
WITH
ORDERS
AND
DIRECTIONS

forthrightly. "I am the boss, not them." And at the end of that week, he left.

We have to pull ourselves and our leadership colleagues out of that mind-set. Employees are not automatons that we program to fill certain functions. When we look at any employee, or even at an applicant, we need to stop and recognize, *This is the kid I used to be. He wants to be inspired by a dream.*

Appreciation but Not Compromise

My call to value the humanness of the employee is in some ways an echo of what God told Moses to say to the ancient Israelites: "Love your neighbor as yourself."[4] Jesus later highlighted this as the second most important commandment.[5]

I've heard speakers apply this to marriage, saying, "Your wife [or husband] is your closest neighbor." Yes, and employees are pretty close too. We work with them every day. When business gets hectic, we sometimes spend more hours with our employees than with our family members. These are people who deserve our respect and our appreciation, even our love.

This does not mean, however, that we go soft on them or compromise our standards. Sometimes the word *love* is misunderstood as softness. If we bend the standards for one employee, putting up with substandard performance or allowing extra time off without justification, the other employees have a right to be upset. So do the owners—the stakeholders—of the firm.

A company's objectives are set for the good of all—the owners, the employees, the public. This positions us to make tough decisions when someone isn't living up to the objectives and, after being dealt with, doesn't mend their ways. We need not worry that we're being "unloving" by holding them to a high standard.

The Well-Oiled Organization

So what makes a company run smoothly and reach its objectives? How do dreams come true in the business world?

Allow me to use a simple diagram:

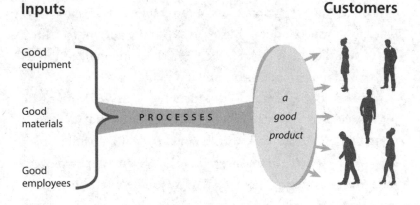

Inputs

Good equipment

Good materials

PROCESSES

Customers

a good product

Good employees

We start, on the left side, with three essential inputs: *good equipment*, *good materials*, and *good employees*.

Let's say you're running a seafood restaurant. First of all, you need a well-equipped kitchen. You need stovetops and ovens that work right, that heat up to the correct temperature, that are easy to control, that are reliable.

Second, you need fresh fish to prepare. If you're offering salmon on the menu, you want the best salmon you can acquire. The same goes for the other kinds of fish you offer.

Third, you need cooks who know how to use the equipment to prepare the salmon, trout, and mahi-mahi to perfection. You need a waitstaff who are efficient and polite to the customers. You need a personable host or hostess at the entrance.

All three of these are vital inputs to your restaurant. And they must be welded together into *processes*—ways of doing things—that result in a superior *product* for the *customers*. What is that product? In the case of the restaurant, it is the sum of the enjoyable dining experience. In my hotel business, it is a restful and pleasant overnight stay. In your business, it will be something else. But the principle remains constant.

Any defect, any shortfall, any disconnection along the way, will spoil the product, sending the customer away unhappy.

For the rest of this chapter, I want to focus on the third input: getting the right employees. We can't just hire anybody. Sometimes if leaders are shorthanded, they can fall into a panic and make decisions they later regret. If the applicant can walk from one end of the room to the other without falling down drunk, they get hired. Soon it becomes apparent that this wasn't a very smart idea.

Jim Collins, the celebrated author of *Good to Great*, was exactly right when he compared us to bus drivers. "Leaders of companies that go from good to great start not with 'where' but with 'who,'" he wrote. "They start by getting the right people on the bus, the wrong people off the bus, and the right people in the right seats."[6]

How do we know who belongs on our "bus" and what "seats" (specific jobs) they should occupy? Is it enough just to run background checks and call their references? Or do we need to do more?

A Cardinal Rule: Don't Just Hire—*Select*

Before you post a single job opening, take time to think about what kind of person could do this job successfully and even joyfully. Who would get up in the morning and *want* to do this? What kind of personality would they have?

I didn't originally know how to go about this, so I asked for help. The consultant firm I chose—Talent Plus in Lincoln, Nebraska—proved to be invaluable. For example, they went to work on "What makes a good doorman?" Interviews with some of our best doormen revealed that they all liked to be outdoors! Blowing snow didn't bother them at all. When we asked about their hobbies, a surprisingly high number of them said "gardening." If I had put them in a windowless room full of computers, they would have been miserable.

Soon we were building what we called a "success profile" for each job category. We started asking applicants for housekeeping positions such questions as, "How do you feel about cleaning up after a party?" Makes sense, doesn't it? If somebody naturally likes to tidy up their home or take care of messes left behind by others, they will do well at cleaning hotel rooms.

For front-desk receptionists, we paid attention to the applicant's personal appearance. Was it important to them to put their best foot forward with strangers? We also wanted to know if they had skills in conflict resolution. "Are you able to cheer people up?" we asked. "When somebody is irritated about something, how do you respond?"

For a salesperson (in our case, someone trying to book conferences, wedding receptions, political dinners, and the like), we measured competitiveness. "Have you ever been part of a winning team?" we wanted to know. We also looked for persuasiveness, as in, "Do you like getting a person to do something they don't want to do?" and "How good are you at getting someone's attention?" In addition, we also sought to measure self-discipline. "Can you keep track of many details at the same time?" we asked.

We found that a lot of people who looked good at first glance were not right for the jobs we had in mind. They didn't belong in that "seat on the bus." We had to carefully *select*. Even to get a good dishwasher, we had to interview at least ten people on average before choosing the right one.

But the reward came as we watched our employee turnover rate drop dramatically. In the hotel and restaurant industry, this can run as high as 120 percent per year, as people decide they don't want to do this kind of work anymore. We got ours down into the 20 percent range. And it wasn't because we paid more. We never became union-organized—we inherited some unionized facilities, but we never were forced to go that route ourselves. We just carefully selected people, and they stayed because they enjoyed what they did. It fit their personality. Meanwhile, their valuable job knowledge didn't just walk out the door. And as a result, we saved a lot of time and money by not having to retrain and retrain and retrain.

Don't Take Shortcuts

As already mentioned, hurry can be a great saboteur. *I've got to have somebody on board by next Monday!* we tell ourselves. Yet all too often, the person we grab to fill a slot doesn't belong there at all. Our momentary sigh of relief in the beginning turns into a groan later on down the road.

I will always regret letting myself get too rushed the year we were incredibly busy, opening eleven new hotels. I needed to hire a general manager for each hotel, of course. I couldn't find enough internal candidates I could promote. So I ended up choosing two men I had worked with in a different company— old friends of mine.

We had done good things together. Both of them were excellent people—honest and hardworking. I ran them through the "success profile" for a general manager. To my dismay, they didn't fit.

I argued with the Talent Plus people in Nebraska. "I'm concerned about your report this time," I said. "Yes, I know you're usually right, but I think you missed something here. I know these guys well. You must have made a mistake."

I had given my organization strict orders that no one should be hired without passing this screening. But I was the boss. I could break my own rule if I wanted to. I hired my two friends anyway.

I am sorry to tell you that two years later, I had to let both of them go. It was very painful. I had tried so hard to salvage them. I had gotten to the point of calling one of them every morning, saying, "How are you doing on this or that? Have you thought about this? If such and such happens, how are you going to mitigate the damage?" It was all for naught.

I lost a lot of sleep over these two situations. But in the end, for the health of the overall company, I had to take action. I had "followed my gut" instead of making a careful, information-based selection. I still feel bad about this years later.

Whose Fault?

In such situations, it is easy to blame the employee who is being dismissed. "Well, Joe just didn't work out," it is said. The leader goes on to think of examples of what Joe did or didn't do that put him in a bad light.

But I have to ask, *Who was the dummy who hired Joe in the first place?* Was Joe actually the right fit for this job? If indeed he was, what could we have done better to make him successful? What did we fail to do? Was it really all his fault?

If we carefully select people and then train them thoroughly (the subject of the next two chapters), these awkward moments should be few and far between. We will be able to experience more moments of sheer joy as we see employees thriving in their work and making strong contributions.

Years ago, I remember meeting a young man named Eby, a refugee from Kenya, on his first day as a dishwasher. I had not directly chosen him; my kitchen manager had done a good job on that particular hire. Some days later, I walked through the kitchen and saw Eby again. "Good morning, sir!" he called out to me. As I greeted him in return, I couldn't help but notice how clean he was, even while doing a messy task.

A couple of weeks later, I saw Eby again. "Good afternoon, sir! How are you today?" Again, his uniform was entirely clean. Even his shoes were polished.

I was curious. I asked the manager, "Tell me about Eby. Does he get the work done? He always looks so clean."

"Mr. Schulze, he gets more done than anybody else. He's just a proud young man. He changes his uniform twice a day!"

This young Kenyan was creating excellence in what he did in that humble station.

Pretty soon, the room service manager said, "I'd like to have him as a waiter." Eby left his water-soaked place to start taking meals up to guests' rooms, collecting tips along the way.

Then the banquet manager said, "I need a banquet captain. Can I have Eby come work for me?"

He kept moving up from there, to the point where today this fellow is the hotel manager of the Ritz-Carlton in downtown Atlanta.

Not everyone is as self-motivated as Eby, I admit. But let's be honest, very few people come to work to be negative or to do a lousy job. People come to contribute to a purpose. When we invite them to join us, to take on positions that befit them, their talents can blossom. We haven't just grabbed them off a shelf to plug an open hole. We haven't treated them, even subconsciously, like a piece of equipment. Instead, we have gotten to know them as human beings and carefully matched their unique interests with a set of tasks that energizes them. As a result, they become employees of excellence for a long, long time, which benefits not only them personally but the organization as well.

CHAPTER SEVEN

FIRST THINGS FIRST

After you've gone through the hard work of evaluating what kind of individual will thrive in a certain position, then interviewed a number of candidates, and finally *selected* (not just hired) the right person for that job, it's time to put them to work, right? You want to get them into the thick of their tasks right away, don't you?

Not so fast.

Orientation is hugely important—but so often it's done badly. On Day One, the manager shakes the new person's hand (after they've spent two hours filling out HR paperwork, having their picture taken, getting their employee badge, and so forth) and says, "Welcome to our department. Glad to have you here. We're a team around here; we all work together." *(Really?)*

"Here, I want you to meet Crystal. She's been with us nine months already. She'll take you around and show you the ropes." *(Hmmm, I didn't know this company was in the rope business.)*

I heard a true story about a new employee who reported for his first shift at a major aeronautics plant, which was a government contractor, in Southern California. The foreman introduced him to the "he'll show you the ropes" employee and then walked away. As soon as the boss was out of earshot, the guy said to the new employee, "Okay. Let me show you how to get through eight hours here without having to do any work. Follow me."

First they toured the break room. Then they checked out the snack bar. Then they visited the parts depot and chatted for a long time with the good-looking woman at the counter. After that, they made various other stops in the plant, until indeed it was time to clock out and go home.

And you wonder why our military jets cost so much?

The Most Important Speech

The most important thing a new employee can learn is not how to tighten a bolt or log into the network or find the first-aid kit on the wall. It is rather to grasp *who we are, what our dreams are,* and *why we exist as an organization.*

Day One is, in fact, a golden moment not to be squandered. Psychologists tell us that human beings rarely take up new behaviors past the age of about sixteen—*unless* they experience a significant emotional event. Otherwise, they just keep doing what they've done before, what their parents and other role models have ingrained in them, reacting in the same ways they've always reacted.

Well, the first day of a new job is a significant emotional event. It's usually a Monday. The person shows up right on time or even early, carefully dressed and all bright-eyed, eager to get started. For the wise leader, it's a *carpe diem* moment—seize the day! The new employee's ears will never be quite this open again, even on the second or third day.

In every new hotel I've opened, I have insisted on doing this orientation myself. If you were a fly on the wall, here is what you would witness.

The room is already abuzz with the new staff members in their seats. I then walk in, wearing my dark business suit and tie.

I approach the lectern. The first words out of my mouth (in my thick German accent) are, "Good morning. My name is Horst Schulze. I am president and COO of this organization, and I am very important around here."

Then I pause while the audience stares at me, wondering what kind of arrogant stuffed shirt this is . . . until I continue. "But so are you! No human being should claim to be superior to the next human being. You are equally as important to this company as I am. Why is that? Because you are going to make a critical contribution here. If I don't show up for work until tomorrow afternoon, few people will notice! But if one of you in housekeeping doesn't show up, the beds won't get made. We won't be able to check in new guests for tomorrow night. The financial hit will be immediate. We will have a disaster on our hands!"

For the rest of that day and the next, I go on unpacking why we do all this, what we think, what is in our heart as an organization. I go through our vision statement, explaining each phrase. I invite each new employee to be part of this vision, explaining what's in it for them personally. "In this way you will be defined as a person of excellence," I say. "The rest of the hospitality industry will see you that way."

Next comes our mission statement, again with full exposition and examples.

I talk a good while about the four objectives that are necessary for any company (as outlined in chapter 3 of this book), expounding on each point. In time I get to these important points:

- "Here is what drives us: we want to be the best in our category . . ."
- "Here is what we believe about customers . . ."

- "Here is what they really want from us: to be cared for, to be treated with dignity, to have their concerns resolved quickly . . ."
- "Here is what 'customer service' means in this organization . . ."
- "Here is what we are all working to achieve. It is what motivates us. This is our passion. So don't do your job just for me or for your supervisor. Join us in pursuing this dream."

I will never forget the impact of this speech when I was opening our first Ritz-Carlton hotel in Montego Bay, Jamaica. I had been previously warned, in fact, by others in the hospitality industry that employees in this country were not good; they were prone to stealing from the company and taking advantage any way they could. It sounded depressing.

I went ahead with my usual orientation on the first day. I invited this roomful of people to be part of our dream. I emphasized that none of them were just "servants." They were going to be ladies and gentlemen serving ladies and gentlemen. "If we can create excellence," I said, "it will be not only to the credit of Ritz-Carlton; it will be to the credit of the country of Jamaica. The hotel guests will go out and spread the word."

Early the next morning, I went for a run alongside the White Witch Golf Course, located next to our facility. Coming back a little after 7:30, I intended to take a quick shower before the meeting, which was slated to start at eight o'clock. To my amazement, I saw people walking toward the hotel dressed in finery. The women were wearing beautiful dresses and were even wearing hats; the men were in their best suits and ties. *Are they headed to some kind of wedding?* I wondered. No, it was too early in the day for that.

I kept watching—until I saw them walking into the employee entrance! These were my new staff members, arriving for the eight o'clock meeting. They had taken to heart my comments of the previous day and had promptly chosen to dress as ladies and gentlemen. It brought tears to my eyes.

"You all look wonderful today!" I said as I stood before them that day. "I am honored that you have come to this meeting so prepared to be ladies and gentlemen in this new work. Please know that you don't have to dress this way every day; we will give you uniforms to wear!"

Next Level

On Wednesday of orientation week, I meet with each department, one at a time, and say, "Now before we open this hotel, let's imagine that your group has a day just to relax, to do something together. What might you do that would be enjoyable? Who has a suggestion?"

In almost every case, someone will say, "We could go on a trip together."

"Sure, that's a good idea," I say. "Where would you like to go for a day trip?"

After discussion, they settle on a nearby attraction of some kind.

"How will you get there and back?" I ask.

The answer is usually to rent a bus for the day.

"Okay, now let me shift gears," I continue. "Your department is starting on a journey. Where do you want to arrive in, say, six months? Where are you headed as a group?"

"Well," people usually respond, "we want to be the best." The wording varies from place to place, but the underlying message is clear.

"Do you all agree on this?" I probe. "Are you sure you want to be the best at what you do?"

"Yes!"

"Okay, now you have your own objective. The other day I talked about the company's objectives. But you're getting more specific. Tell me what 'being the best' means to you."

Answers rise up: "We want to be the cleanest." "We want to be the friendliest." "We want to be the most efficient." "We want to be respected." As they talk, I write their answers on a flip chart.

And then I'll often interject, "Along with all these, don't you want to have fun too?"

"Oh yes—that too!"

Eventually I ask the department manager to stand up. "Here is your leader," I say. "Do you know what his role is? I'll tell you: his role is to help you do the things you've just listed. He will help you achieve the department objectives.

"And sometimes that will mean not allowing you to settle for less than what you've outlined here. If, for example, you hear him saying, 'Hey, folks, we're not being the cleanest, like we said we were going to be,' don't get upset with him. He is merely calling you back to your overall goal of being the best. And if he notices that someone is not interested in helping your group reach that goal, part of his job is to weed that person out. You're on a mission, and no one can be allowed to sabotage that."

IF THE CULTURE OF YOUR ORGANIZATION ISN'T RIGHT IT WILL **DEVOUR** YOUR BEST-LAID PLANS

Only on Thursday of orientation week do we finally get down to "the ropes"—the details of how to perform a particular function, what safety measures must be followed, what reports must be filled out, and so forth. But ahead of all that comes the big picture, the purpose we are all striving to fulfill. As I said, it's best if they hear it directly from me. In the case of an existing hotel rather than a new one, however, the general manager will do a similar orientation—and keep doing it with every new crop of employees month after month.

I am not saying that you have to do things my way in your organization. You can create your own process. But whatever you do, give your grand purpose the spotlight it deserves—in a setting and at a time when your employees are paying the closest attention.

Orientation must never become routine—a chore to be endured, a box to be checked off. It is crucial for establishing the platform on which all future success can be built. Without it or with only a shortchanged version of it, the organization will be forever hobbled.

The great business genius Peter Drucker is reported to have said, "Culture eats strategy for breakfast."[1] In other words, you can write up all the strategies and directives and systems you want, but if the culture of your organization isn't right, it will devour your best-laid plans. You won't have a living, synchronized team; you'll have only a bureaucracy. But when you create a focused, energized culture—starting on Day One—your organization can thrive for years and decades to come.

CHAPTER EIGHT

WHY REPETITION IS A GOOD THING

The most inspiring speech, the slickest PowerPoint display, the greatest video presentation—all of these tend to fade over the following twenty-four hours. No matter how great and thorough an employee's orientation, it won't stick without ongoing reinforcement.

Do you know what Coca-Cola is? Of course, you do. Then why do they keep advertising their product? Because the company wants to stay in the front of your brain. They spend $4 billion every year to keep from slipping into the shadows.

The process of building great employees involves four things: first, initial *selection*; next, inspiring *orientation*; then, initial *teaching* of specific job functions; and finally, *sustaining what has been taught*. This requires a conscious system that is diligently pursued.

Ten Minutes a Day

When I tell you how we did this at the Ritz-Carlton and then at the Capella Hotel Group, you may think it's overkill. But it worked. I instituted a short stand-up meeting *at the beginning of every shift* (remember, hotels run around the clock) to focus on one of our twenty-four Service Standards. The leader reads the standard, makes comments about what it means, and maybe tells a story or reads a relevant customer comment to show the standard in action. Employees may add their own input. Then they head off to their individual assignments.

If today covers no. 1, tomorrow will deal with no. 2, the next day with no. 3, and so forth. After twenty-four days, the cycle begins again.

I wrote the Service Standards to fit the hospitality industry, but they can be readily adapted to other lines of business. Here they are:

1. The Canon states the purpose for us to be in business and is shared within the organization.

   What is the Canon, you may ask? It is the formal statement that we "are in business to create value and unparalleled results for our owners by creating products which fulfill individual customer expectations. We deliver reliable, genuinely caring, and timely service superior to our competition, with respected and empowered employees who work in an environment of belonging and purpose. We are supportive and contributing members of society, operating with uncompromising values, honor, and integrity." Obviously, there's a lot to digest there!

2. The *Zeitgeist* is known, owned, and energized by all. It is the cornerstone of our service commitment to our guests.

   What is the *Zeitgeist*, you may ask? It's a good German word (!) that means "spirit of the time [or season]." It is guest-driven, since guests' desires can change over time. The subsections of the *Zeitgeist* are exclusivity, loyalty, experience, and legacy—each of which we define in its own sentence.

3. Our Service Process (i.e., the warm welcome, the compliance with and anticipation of guests' needs, and the fond farewell) is followed for all guest interactions—not just some, but all.

4. We assist each other, stepping out of our primary duties to effectively provide service to our guests.

5. Answer the telephone within three rings and with a smile in your voice. Use terminology that reflects Capella's image. Do not screen calls. Avoid call transfers and placing guests on hold.

6. You are responsible for identifying and immediately correcting defects before they affect a guest. Defect prevention is key to service excellence.

7. Ensure that all areas of the hotel are immaculate. We are responsible for cleanliness, maintenance, and organization. Each hotel follows our established C.A.R.E. program ("Clean And Repair Everything"—whether it shows to the public or not).

8. Always recognize guests. Interrupt whatever activity you are doing when a guest is within three meters (ten feet); greet them with a smile and offer assistance.

9. Safety and security are everyone's responsibility. Know your role in an emergency situation and in protecting guest and hotel assets. Report unsafe conditions or security concerns immediately, and correct them if possible.

For example, if a suitcase seems to be left unattended in the lobby, staff must find out what is going on. For a more serious example, every maid knows that if a "Do Not Disturb" sign is still hanging on a doorknob by early afternoon, the room needs to be checked. Most likely the guest had simply forgotten to bring the placard inside—but what if someone died overnight? (It has happened, more than once.) The maid will knock on the door, and if no one answers, she will notify security personnel, who will check the computer to see who and how many guests are registered to this room. Then they will try to phone the room, asking, "Is everything all right? Can we be of service to you?" If no one picks up the line, they will come with a master pass to open the door—and if the door chain is still hooked, they will use a bolt cutter to gain entrance. Hopefully, there hasn't been a tragedy inside.

10. We all have a responsibility to participate in the elimination of defects in our work area for continuous improvement.

   In other words, don't assume "somebody else" will take care of that. If there's a spillage on a floor, respond right away to get it cleaned up as quickly as possible so someone doesn't slip and fall. In one of our early hotels, a housekeeper noticed that a bathrobe kept showing up on the floor. She thought to herself, *Well, why don't we have a hook on the wall right by the shower? We should.* Soon a hook was installed in every room of that hotel and throughout the entire chain.

11. When a guest encounters difficulty, you are responsible to own it and start the problem resolution process. You are empowered to resolve any problem to the guest's complete satisfaction. Follow the QIAF process (Quality Improvement Action Form) to properly document issues.

12. Escort guests until they are comfortable with the directions or make visual contact with their destination. Do not point.

13. Always give guests your complete attention and focus. Be responsive, caring, and timely in providing service.

    To be specific, no glancing down at your computer screen, your watch, your cell phone, and so forth.

14. Be respectful of our guests' personal time and privacy, delivering service that does not interrupt or interfere with our guests' activities. Never approach a guest to request a favor, such as an autograph—or a selfie, for that matter!

15. The Capella experience is memorable and unique. Be proactive, finding ways to surprise and delight our guests.

16. Be sensitive and adjust to the guests' style, pace, situation, and each unique environment to create a personal experience for them.

    For example, we would not treat the board chairman of the Bank of England the way we would treat a young family from Texas.

    We once had a guest with two energetic boys who played hockey in the hallway with their toy plastic hockey sticks and puck. Well, we couldn't allow this to continue, of course. But instead of just ordering them to stop, we said to them, "Guess what, we have a meeting room that's not being used today. We'll clear out the chairs to make an open space, and you can play hockey there!" The problem was solved, and everyone was happy. In contrast, some guests are more formal and reserved.

17. Our appearance, grooming, and demeanor represent Capella. Our attire and personal image are appropriate and impeccable. We avoid words that are inconsistent with Capella's image, such as "hi," "okay," "no problem," "guys," and so forth.

18. The suggested hours of operation are guidelines, not limitations, for satisfying individual guest desires and preferences.

    In other words, don't say, "Too bad, the pool is closed now" or "Sorry, my shift is over." Keep doing whatever it takes to serve the guest.

19. We are empowered and required to fulfill our guests' needs. Identify their unique requirements and preferences both prior to the arrival and during their stay in order to individualize their experience.

    We once had a guest with an odd request. He wanted seven boxes of tissue in his room! The first time he stayed with us, we failed to provide them. When he came back another time with the same request, we finally woke up and did what he asked from that point on. We wondered if he had some kind of allergy, but it was not our business to figure it out.

Where it gets really extreme is when movie stars come to your hotel. Their people send pages and pages of dos and don'ts—in one case, nineteen pages, two-sided! Entertainers, for some reason, will ask for a total blackout of the windows. They want absolute darkness for sleeping. So in addition to taping the edges of the shades to the window trim, we even had to tape over the little electronic lights on the appliances in the room! One entertainer specified, "No vacuuming of the corridor before one o'clock in the afternoon." Well, okay!

20. Knowledge is essential to create the Capella experience for our guests. Know all hotel services and signature activities, along with local features, history, and traditions.

As one leader of a nonprofit organization put it to his staff, "The *worst* thing you can say to a constituent is 'I don't know. Ask somebody else.'"

21. Confidentiality at Capella is paramount. Never speak to the press or anyone outside our company concerning the hotel and guests. If you are approached for information, please notify your general manager.

Sorry, news reporters and gossip columnists!

22. Be positive both inside and outside the workplace. It is our responsibility to create a great environment and reputation for our hotel and each other.

I am not embarrassed at all to say to employees, "We expect you to be loyal. This is where you make your living. I want you to say nothing but positive things about your fellow workers and the hotel in general—here at work and when you're away from work as well. Don't forget, the way you describe this workplace is a reflection on you personally too."

23. All forms of our written communication (signage, letters, emails, handwritten notes, and so forth) reflect this hotel's image.

That is because *everything* communicates. If the restaurant menu has a smudge on it, it says that maybe the kitchen is not clean either. If there's a misspelled word, it shows carelessness. Maybe ninety-nine guests out of a hundred won't notice, but we want to keep all one hundred guests coming back and trusting us.

24. As service professionals, we are always gracious and treat our guests and each other with respect and dignity.

Notice that it says not only "guests," but also "each other." You can't turn graciousness and kindness on or off with a switch, depending on whether a guest is within earshot. I have noticed that in hiring, applicants will often say they hope for "a great work environment." Well, who creates that? We *all* do, and the way we treat each other is a big factor.

Throughout the hotel industry, there's a common term for the interior spaces and procedures called "the back of the house." We don't allow that term. Instead, we say, "the heart of the house." As we look each other in the eye, greet each other positively, and support each other, we create our own environment that both we and the guests will appreciate.

When a staff member hears these things again and again and again, twelve or more times a year, they sink in deeply. Employees carry the little fold-up card in their pocket for reference if needed. It becomes second nature to obey these Service Standards without debate. *This is just the way we do things around here*, they think to themselves.

Why Keep Repeating

You may be thinking to yourself, *Oh my goodness, we're too busy to keep hammering this kind of thing again and again. We have deadlines to meet! Our business just runs at too fast a pace for this.*

That's what I heard more than once from my own investors in the early days. "What do you mean ten minutes every day?" asset managers would say. "Do you know how many hours that is? You're wasting payroll dollars."

My response was simple: "So do you want me to keep them stupid about their jobs? Is that what you want? These ten minutes are among the most important of the entire shift."

The truth is, this was standard procedure in the fine European hotels where I got my start. I still remember the manager or the maître d' lining us up to give us instructions—as well as to check us out visually! Were our fingernails clean? Were our shoes shined? Was our hair combed and neat? Were our uniforms pressed and spotless? No one was allowed to serve guests without first passing inspection.

When I came to America and eventually had the opportunity to organize Ritz-Carlton, I introduced the lineup to accomplish several objectives. First and foremost, I wanted every employee at every level to know, understand, commit to, and live the company's values. Bitter experience in previous companies had taught me that a onetime orientation speech was not enough.

Second, I wanted to reinforce brand consistency. We were a young, rapidly growing, constantly changing, and geographically spread-out organization. Were the Ritz-Carlton guests in Shanghai or Osaka getting the same treatment as those in Atlanta or Laguna Niguel? The lineup provided a means to ensure that every day, every employee on every shift in every location received the same message.

Third, there would always be new employees. Turnover in my industry was high. I needed a way to keep teaching them what we were all about. I wanted to minimize the messy "he said; no he didn't" arguments:

"Hey, you're supposed to be doing the task this way."

"I never heard that."

"Sure you did; they told us in orientation."

"Not the class I was in."

This doesn't happen when everyone is hearing the same message at the same time repeatedly—and when the messages are printed on cards that every employee carries!

Fourth, many hospitality workers have a limited education. Many are immigrants, and some do not read or write English. Learning in a classroom setting is often ineffective or even intimidating. They're more comfortable assembling in a corner or along a hallway of a work area for a few minutes at the beginning of their shift. There they can listen better and even find the confidence to ask questions or contribute ideas.

Finally, the lineup gives management a chance to let employees know what's going on throughout the company—the new ventures, the promotions, the good news as well as the problems or challenges being faced. This helps them align themselves with the organization's thinking and objectives. Otherwise, they work in a narrow tunnel, just doing their assigned tasks and having no idea what the bigger picture looks like.

Do you remember Stephen Covey's point in his bestseller *The 7 Habits of Highly Effective People* about the difference between "urgent" and "important"? On the one hand, urgent things, he said, are the phone calls, interruptions, and even some meetings that gobble up daily life. Important things, on the other hand, are planning, relationship building, and recognizing new opportunities.

Covey even drew a little chart with four boxes to show the relative importance. "As long as you focus on Quadrant I [a list of urgent things, like crises and problems]," he wrote, "it keeps getting bigger and bigger until it dominates you. It's like the pounding surf. A huge problem comes and knocks you down and you're wiped out. You struggle back up only to face another one that knocks you down and slams you to the ground."

Covey went on to write, "Quadrant II [the things that aren't necessarily urgent but are nevertheless important] is the heart of effective personal management [and, I might add, organizational management]. It deals with things that are not urgent, but are important. It deals with . . . all those things we know we need to do, but somehow seldom get around to doing, because they aren't urgent."

Covey summed up his thoughts on Quadrant II, "Whether you are a student at the university, a worker in an assembly line, a homemaker . . . or president of a company, I believe that if you were to ask what lies in Quadrant II and cultivate the proactivity to go after it . . . your effectiveness would increase dramatically.

Your crises and problems would shrink to manageable proportions because you would be thinking ahead."[1]

Diligent, repeated, sustained reinforcement of your standards lies at the heart of Quadrant II. This means you work on the important things, not just the urgent things.

The Ripple Benefits

Over the years, I have convinced a number of other companies to implement this kind of daily reinforcement. Some of them call it a "huddle." They have written their own standards to fit their situation, of course. But they recognize, as I do, that if they intend to be the leader in their market segment, they need to keep reinforcing what makes them number one. Otherwise, it will slip.

Shortly after our company took over a New York City hotel that needed improvement, one of the first things I noticed was the absence of staff meetings to train and sustain their practices. I had actually moved into the hotel for three months to see what was really going on—or rather *not* going on. I started daily stand-up meetings, as described above.

One day I said, "Okay, somebody tell a good story from what happened yesterday."

A housekeeper spoke up. "There's a little girl who lives with her mother in room such and such. I had found out it was her birthday. So I stopped on the way to work yesterday and bought her a little doll. She was very happy."

"Wow, you did that?" I exclaimed, as everybody applauded. "That's wonderful! First of all, I'm going to reimburse you for the cost of the doll. And second, we have a tradition you may not

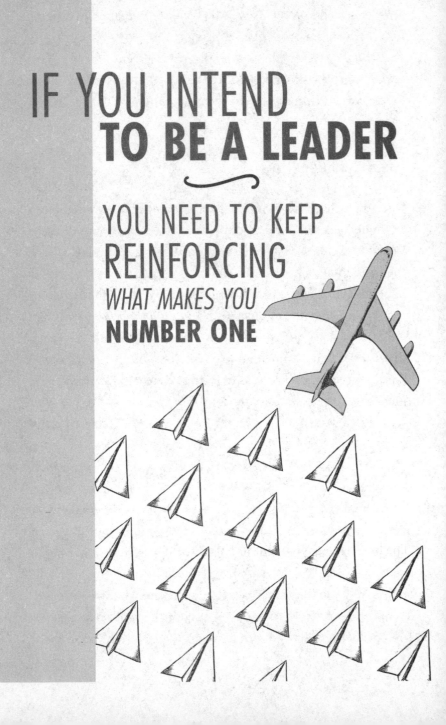

IF YOU INTEND
TO BE A LEADER

YOU NEED TO KEEP
REINFORCING
WHAT MAKES YOU
NUMBER ONE

know about; it's called 'Lightning Strikes.' When somebody on the team does something extraordinary, we zap them with $50. You'll be getting that soon!"

Another housekeeper (a Burmese immigrant) noticed one of her long-term guests running low on a certain brand of toothpaste. She told me about it and asked, "Can I go buy her another tube?"

"Absolutely," I said. "Here's the money. Go to the drugstore next door and do it right away."

These are the kinds of gestures that turn *satisfied* customers into *loyal* customers. They realize that people are watching out for them, anticipating their needs and wants—a case of Service Standard no. 15 in action. We're taking good service to the next level (personalization).

And meanwhile, employees feel energized and empowered. They're not just a cog in a big machine. They're using their creativity to help make the company better and stronger.

Continuous Improvement

The more a staff interacts, talking to each other and supporting one another, the more smoothly the operation goes. This is part of working on our efficiencies (Objective Number Four mentioned earlier). In the very first Ritz-Carlton we opened in the Buckhead section of Atlanta, we served tea in the afternoons. The local women liked the ambience of stopping by to chat with their friends, listen to the live piano music, and have tea together. They loved the beautiful Wedgwood china cups and serving pots. I knew I wasn't making any money on this (each cup cost $100!), but it definitely set an image of elegance.

However, there was a small problem. We kept getting complaints about lukewarm tea. (That's what you call a *defect* in your product.) Everyone who complained to the waiter was provided with another, hotter cup of tea, of course. That cost more money and additional time, plus the next guests didn't get served as promptly. Meanwhile, every woman who told her friends about the lukewarm tea was undercutting the reputation I was trying to establish among the public.

I could have called in the food and beverage manager and scolded him. "What's the matter with you? Stop serving cold tea!" And he could have gone back to his workers and yelled at them, "This is unacceptable!" But it wouldn't have solved the problem. It would only have left everyone in a bad frame of mind.

The better way was to say to the staff together at the end of a stand-up meeting, "We're all committed to our high standard of meeting and even exceeding customer expectations. So let's look into why the afternoon tea is coming out lukewarm."

Sure enough, they discovered the problem—the cups were being stored right up against the ice machine! No wonder the tea was lukewarm. It was an easy thing to change.

We had another challenge with the teapots. The spouts kept breaking off. At $200 apiece, these were expensive replacements! Again, we went to the staff and said, "Why do these expensive teapots keep breaking? Let's find out."

Soon the dishwashing people were showing how the teapots moved along a belt toward the machine until they reached a trigger point, where a bar would stop their motion. And if they happened to put the teapot on the belt with the spout forward—*snap!* So they fashioned a piece of soft rubber hose to place over each spout heading into the washing process. Suddenly, the breakages stopped.

Neither the manager nor I would have ever figured this out by ourselves. We had to give the workers room to analyze and then solve the problem. They didn't *want* to keep serving cold tea or breaking teapots. They wanted to do the job right. They understood the need to save money and be more efficient. So they found solutions as we involved them in a couple of processes that needed attention.

If some corporate accountant had shot off a memo that read, "We don't understand why your costs are so high!" a typical manager might have replied, "Well, why do we have expensive Wedgwood china in the first place? Let's just buy cheaper stuff—$10 pots and $2 cups." What would have been the result of these cost-cutting measures? Degradation of the guest experience. A lowering of our brand below the competition.

Good leaders don't do this. They keep their eyes on the goal of having the finest tea experience in town. This requires asking employees to help find real answers for defects that show up. Because of the common commitment to high standards—*reinforced on a continuing basis*—the organization steadily moves forward.

CHAPTER NINE

MANAGERS PUSH; LEADERS INSPIRE

Organizational leaders all over the world instinctively assume that many of their employees are reluctant donkeys who need a shove from behind, while only a minority are motivated to get moving on their own initiative.

The leaders might not put it this bluntly, of course. But deep down inside, it's how they're thinking. They assume this is just the burden of leadership.

Thankfully, we've gotten past the days of snarling slave drivers with whips. Methods to raise productivity have gotten more nuanced in our time. But is this really the best we can do? Who will do a better job—the employee who "has to" because the boss is breathing down his neck or the employee who *wants* to do the job? Obviously, it would be the latter.

Once you or I take an employee on board, it is our job to lead them to *want* to be connected to the overall goal. As more people, from the lowest ranks to the highest, understand customer desires and want to meet them efficiently, our overall success will swell—and our personal heartburn will lessen.

What I Believe

I believe we were all made with two fundamental desires: (1) purpose and (2) relationship. We're not designed to flounder aimlessly through life. We're hardwired to want to do something of value. It may be anything from painting a picture to building a toolshed to flying to the moon. We've been programmed to seek to achieve in some area so we can look back with pride and say, "I did that." Along the way, we crave relationships with other human beings. We want to connect, to talk, to be heard, to interact, to gain new ideas, to help another person, and, yes, even to love.

The task of any business leader is to accept these two realities and channel them into his or her work. I like what James Autry, former president of the Meredith Corporation (publisher of a dozen or more national magazines), wrote in one of his books:

Business, like art and science, has been revealed and conceived through the intellect and imagination of people, and it develops or declines because of the intellect and imagination of people.

In fact, there is no business; there are only people. Business exists only *among* people and *for* people.

Seems simple enough, and it applies to every aspect of business, but not enough businesspeople seem to get it.

Reading the economic forecasts and the indicators and the ratios and the rates of this or that, someone from another planet might actually believe that there really are invisible hands at work in the marketplace.

It's easy to forget what the measurements are measuring. Every number—from productivity rates to salaries—is just a device contrived by people to measure the results of the enterprise of other people. For managers, the most important job is not measurement but motivation. And you can't motivate numbers.[1]

That last sentence deserves to be put in bold type and capital letters. We who lead businesses and organizations are not in the numbers game! We're in the people game—dealing with customers, employees, colleagues, owners, and all the rest for the best possible outcomes.

If you don't believe people have a bedrock yearning for purpose and relationship, then you may turn into something very dark—an exploiter of people. Your days, weeks, months, and years become one power play after another, taking advantage of every chance you get to extract talent and money for your own benefit. People quickly come to distrust you. Their opportunities to blossom, to be excellent in what they do, are squeezed time and again. They begin to shrivel on the inside, or else they run away to a healthier environment.

I will go so far as to draw this distinction: *managers push; leaders inspire.* If you are just shoving and watchdogging and reprimanding your employees, don't call yourself a leader. Stop and ask yourself how you can change to be an *inspiration* to those in your charge.

Beyond Pep Talk

Inspiring employees to have a positive attitude about their work does not, however, mean resorting to rah-rah language and euphemisms. In fact, such verbiage can work against us, causing cynicism. You may remember your high school days of reading George Orwell's famous novel *1984*, with its Newspeak vocabulary of terms such as *joycamp*—in actuality, a grim forced-labor camp.

Here are just a few examples from today's organizational jargon:

- *"We're a team!"* That is, of course, a very good idea—*if* the team members are unified around a common objective. A football team exists for a greater purpose than just wearing special uniforms and high-fiving each other. Its whole point is to cross the goal line and get into the end zone more times than the opponent. Each player has a role to play in helping make that happen. A team also lives by certain rules. They have to show up for practices at the appointed times. They have to memorize the playbook. They have to do what the coach requires.

  Bosses who flippantly roll out the "team speech" without an underlying objective or set of expectations that everyone understands and embraces are just wasting their breath.

  Have you ever wondered why people choose to retire? Too many times it is because they've spent a lifetime working but never sensing that their effort contributed to anything meaningful. They just spent their time at work occupying a function. And now they're eager to get out of that box.

- *"You're all associates!"* This is the new upgrade term for *employee*. My question is, "Associated to what?" Does the person have any sense of being tied into something larger, integrated into a cause or goal? If not, it won't matter what their clip-on name tag says.

  I can't tell you how many times I've consulted at a company where everyone was called an "associate" and randomly asked, "So, what's the objective of this company?

What are you associated to?"—only to get blank stares. People couldn't frame any kind of coherent response. They had no idea.

- *"We're a family!"* The term *family* is a very precious, deeply emotional word. It brings up feelings of love, safety, caring, protection, enrichment, identity, and heritage. Even if someone's family of origin was not the healthiest, they still carry within their hearts a notion of what they *wish* their home had been like.

  For a workplace to call itself a family is to stake a lofty claim. It means the people here truly care about each other, look out for one another's interests, seek to develop one another's talents, and believe the best about their coworkers. Until this is a reality, the word is not suitable. When companies hold summer picnics and Christmas parties, they are making headway at creating a sense of belonging. That is a good start—and much more can be done to encourage a true family setting.

- *"We believe in alignment!"* Company leaders talk about this constantly. But when I sit with them, they don't even know what alignment is. It's not just making staff members stand in line. I've been in front of groups where I gave them seven minutes to write down what their company was all about, and their answers were all over the map. It was pathetic.

  In a truly aligned organization, everybody down to the newest employee knows the firm's objectives and motives. They know where the company wants to go. They have heard where the value is for them personally. They know the expectation of the customer and how to respond to the situations they encounter.

- *"We are committed to empowerment!"* This promise appeals to everyone's deep yearning. Nobody wants to feel powerless; they crave having the ability to make a difference in the world. They want to use their minds, not just their hands and feet. They want the organization to trust them to act in its best interest. But if they spend ten cents of the company's money and have to write up a report on where it went, they don't feel very empowered. They can tell that the system doesn't trust them to make an intelligent decision. They're not really part of moving the enterprise forward; they're just a cog in the wheel.

- *"We have an open-door policy!"* On the face of it, this signifies that you can approach the boss at any time and talk about any subject. You don't have to flatter him or her; you can speak your mind. But in far too many companies, employees don't dare to raise sticky issues. They fear retaliation. They've heard stories about what happened to the last whistleblower. Better to keep their mouths shut. The door may be open, but few brave souls get up the nerve to darken it.

  The popularity of the TV show *Undercover Boss* is built on leaders taking the initiative to leave their corner offices and find out what's really happening on the sales floor or the job site. There they hear employees unintentionally spill things that have needed to be said for a long time. No wonder viewers enjoy watching this show. Many no doubt wish they could speak with this much frankness to *their* supervisors.

- *"Our company is B2B!* [business-to-business]" Yes, but the businesses to which you sell your goods or services are composed of real live human beings—people with likes and dislikes, feelings and opinions, wishes and aspirations.

They hold the keys as to whether or not to keep doing business with you. If, for example, you manufacture semiconductor chips to sell to Hewlett-Packard, Dell, or Toshiba, you're involved in more than just manipulating silicon in a sterile room. Chips don't talk to motherboards. You are making something that you want a company of human beings to purchase for their end products, which they want other human beings in the marketplace to choose for their homes or workplaces.

Business is just a summary word for this multilevel set of very human exchanges. Technical jargon must not obscure this.

The words used by leaders must be thoughtfully chosen, not just silly slogans thrown around. Otherwise, employees feel disrespected. Talk can be cheap; what counts is the meaning behind the words. Used properly, words can be the glue that unites an organization into true and effective teamwork.

Grasping the "Why"

Employees are not usually inspired to work hard for someone else's purpose—for example, to drive up the yearly dividend or to make the boss look good to his or her superiors. What really gets them going is *their own purpose*. If that purpose aligns with what the organization cares about, then it's a win-win for everyone.

What do employees care about deep down inside? Earning a living, of course—but more than that, they care about being respected, about feeling useful, about looking at the work they've done and being able to call it "excellent." In an article in the *Harvard Business Review*, Harvard Business School professor Clayton Christensen wrote, "One of the theories that gives great insight on . . . how to be sure we find happiness in our careers is from Frederick Herzberg [the brilliant business psychologist from half a century ago], who asserts that the powerful motivator in our lives isn't money; it's the opportunity to learn, grow in responsibilities, contribute to others, and be recognized for achievements."[2]

Christensen echoed that perspective in his own conclusion in the article: "Management is the most noble of professions if it's practiced well. No other occupation offers as many ways to help others learn and grow, take responsibility and be recognized for achievement, and contribute to the success of a team . . . Doing deals doesn't yield the deep rewards that come from building up people. I want students to leave my classroom knowing that."[3]

Sure, money plays a role in employee motivation. You can't get by if you pay workers fifty cents an hour less than your competition. But this isn't the biggest factor. More important is being part of a worthwhile dream. When it comes right down to it, the vast majority of people in this world want to excel at something. They just need a context in which to do so. They look to us as leaders to provide that setting.

When I was growing up in Germany, a man named Wilhelm Furtwängler was arguably the greatest symphony conductor of the century. His Berlin Philharmonic was incredible. He bravely stayed in Germany through almost all of World War II, giving the Nazis fits because he wouldn't endorse their vile ideology. He refused to give the Nazi salute or to sign his letters "Heil Hitler!" like everyone else. The Reich would like to have gotten rid of him, but they didn't dare, because his music was so revered.

Years later, I saw a television interview of an American musician who, after the war ended, rushed to Germany to get hired in this man's orchestra. He was asked to describe the experience.

"Let me recall the first day," he replied. "I was standing in the back of the rehearsal hall studying my score, since I was due to join the next set. But I could not concentrate; I realized I had never heard music like that. It went to a level I didn't think was humanly possible. It gave me chills. I looked closer and saw that it was not an assistant conducting the rehearsal; it was Furtwängler."

This musician did not cross the ocean from America to Germany for a paycheck. It was all for the soaring thrill of excellence.

Great leaders hold great expectations, which they will not compromise. But this does not deter their followers. Yes, the followers may sigh sometimes and say it's hard to please the leader, but in their hearts they know it is worth the effort. They, too, want to be the best. And they want their family and friends to admire them as a result.

Finding the Right Touch

Inspiring people to rise to excellence can be complicated at times, because individuals are not all alike. I remember an assistant restaurant manager at one of my first jobs as a department leader at the Hyatt Regency in Chicago. He was a sharp young man, but he just wasn't getting the work done to my satisfaction. And in my inexperience, I came down on him pretty intensely. We had more than one go-around in my office. Things reached a point where one day I said to my peers in a staff meeting, "I'm going to let him go."

"Really?" said the rooms manager. "Would you mind if I took him on instead? I think he'd do well at the front desk."

"Go ahead if you want to," I answered. "I just think he's the wrong guy for us."

Well, in fact, the young man worked out great in his new role. I had to say to myself, *Where did I fail?* I had pushed him too hard, not realizing that he needed a lighter touch. Under different leadership, he was doing fine. In fact, he went on to even greater responsibilities in the hotel industry.

I would have done better to have quietly taken him aside and asked him questions: "What do you think about what happened yesterday? Did this reflect our motto of 'Ladies and Gentlemen Serving Ladies and Gentlemen'? How could this event have come to a better outcome?" I have no doubt now, with hindsight, that he would have come up with good answers.

James Autry says it well: "Good management is largely a matter of love. Or if you're uncomfortable with that word, call it caring, because proper management involves caring for people, not manipulating them."[4]

It Pays Off

As the years go by, I'm gratified to see people like that young man doing well, whether I inspired them properly or not. I enjoy seeing former employees spread out across the industry in key roles.

Not long ago, I attended a grand reopening for a hotel in Bali, Indonesia, that used to be a Ritz-Carlton. Now the owners had asked Capella to come in and manage it instead. There was a massive reception with hundreds of important people present—politicians, village leaders, tour operators, travel agents, you name it. I was invited to give a little speech about our dreams for the future of this establishment.

Afterward, a shy, young Indonesian waited around to talk to me. "Do you have a minute, Mr. Schulze? I know you are a very busy man."

"Yes, of course you can talk to me," I replied.

"Mr. Schulze, I was a banquet waiter when you opened this hotel as a Ritz-Carlton," he began. "I was at the orientation you did, standing at the back and listening carefully. And after you left, I came up and took the flip charts you had drawn. I went home and studied them again. I can still repeat every word you said. Now I am the general manager of a hotel in Ubud [one of Bali's most famous tourist destinations], up in the mountains. I just want to thank you."

What a fulfilling moment for me. It made my day—or even more so, it made my year. As I reflected later, I thought back to how that first maître d' had inspired me as a teenager to care for guests. Now history was repeating itself. Herr Zeitler had never concentrated on the number of guests or the size of their checks. From him I had learned not to focus on the dollars, but to focus instead on the things that *make* the dollars.

Whenever I do an orientation, I always pray that at least one person will "get it"—that they'll take what I've said and internalize it and then go out and apply it for their future. In this case, that prayer was answered.

Inspiring employees is vital to an organization's success. And sometimes it bears more fruit than we could ever imagine.

CHAPTER TEN

BRIDGING THE GULF BETWEEN MANAGEMENT AND LABOR

Even after all I've written in the past chapters about leaders and employees banding together around a common vision, uniting to pursue a great purpose, some of you may still be skeptical. *Nice theory, Horst,* you may be thinking, *but in my situation, it's just not gonna happen. The two outlooks are fundamentally different.*

Too many bad memories may arise of workers pushing for something (more money, more days off, better benefits) that management believes will hurt the bottom line. Conflict and resentment ensue. The rise of labor unions in the early twentieth century (and some even earlier) is evidence of this hostility. But even in nonunion situations, a thin layer of politeness can cover a deep reservoir of animosity.

Is this just the way life has to be?

A Place to Belong

I've had decades of experience working with labor unions, particularly the HERE (Hotel Employees and Restaurant Employees International Union, which has now merged into a larger group known as UNITE HERE). I've had plenty of time to think about why unions thrive. I've come to see that it's because they give workers a community of common interest—when the employer is failing to do so. The ordinary worker says, "Here is a group I

A THIN LAYER OF POLITENESS

CAN COVER A DEEP RESERVOIR
OF ANIMOSITY

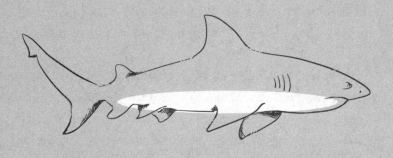

can identify with. They care about me, even if the boss doesn't seem to." The union fills an emotional vacuum.

Notice that the very word used—*union*—speaks of togetherness, camaraderie, commonality. Some of the biggest unions evoke the same sentiment when they call themselves the International *Brotherhood* of Electrical Workers (IBEW) or the *United* Auto Workers (UAW).

This simply shows that people want to feel a part of something. If they don't feel part of the organization's dream, they will gravitate toward the union's dream, which is to stand up for workers' rights and benefits.

I remember taking over a hotel in New York City, a heavily unionized town. It wasn't that great a facility, and my initial employee survey showed job satisfaction at just above 50 percent. Naturally, with this prevailing attitude among the workers, customer satisfaction wasn't much better—a bit above 60 percent.

The general manager I hired did a great job building a new frame of mind, inviting employees to imagine what this hotel could become. How can we rise to excellence here in the tough New York City market? How can we make a new name for ourselves?

Two years later, employee satisfaction was at 90 percent, and customer satisfaction was at 92 percent. In the meantime, the collective bargaining agreement had come up for renewal. The employees insisted that our "Credo," with its twenty-four Service Standards (described in chapter 8), become part of the new contract! They were saying, *This is who we are. This is what our hotel is about. We want this to be documented in the next contract.*

When we planted a new hotel in San Francisco—another union stronghold—we opened up without a union agreement.

Picketers arrived right away. They kept marching in front of our building *for three years*, during which time they forced an election on whether to organize. Our employees turned the union down. They didn't feel they needed it.

This was not because we were paying them that much better than the union hotels in the city. Our pay rates were pretty much the same as the rest. It was rather the sense of belonging that the workers felt. They were already feeling a part of something that made them proud.

Learning to "Play Ball"

The stiffest resistance I ever encountered was when Hyatt sent me to Pittsburgh (home of the United Steelworkers) to take over a dilapidated Howard Johnson hotel that Hyatt had just acquired. Average nightly occupancy was below 30 percent. I'll never forget my first walk-through on a warm Monday in June, when a doorman called out to me, "Hey, come over here!"

I walked toward him and saw his name tag: *Jim.*

"You know what I do here?" he said.

"Yes, you're a doorman to greet the guests," I answered.

He opened up his right hand to reveal something I would never have expected: a roll of pennies! "I keep this here inside my hand," he explained, "so that if I need to crack somebody in the face, I'll break their jaw!"

I swallowed hard. "That's interesting," I said. "I guess I didn't know it would have that effect."

But in that moment, I noticed two or three holes in Jim's uniform that the hotel supplied him. I had to say to myself,

What can I expect from this man when management gives him a uniform with holes?

The only other comment I recall from that conversation was when Jim said, "Look, if you play ball with us, you'll be okay."

"Well," I answered, "I'm here for no other reason than you are—to do a good job. So yes, let's play ball together by doing a good job for the owners, the guests, and you the employees." I walked away promising myself that someday Jim would click his heels when he saw me.

Just a few hours later in my office, my new secretary informed me in a worried tone that the union was coming to see me. Sure enough, in walked a group of five men with stern faces. The leader of the group—a burly fellow I'll call Walter, the union's regional vice president—deliberately turned his chair around so he could face away from me. It was like a scene out of a movie.

Walter set the tone right away by saying to the guy next to him, "Ask him if he's ever seen a car blow up."

I didn't wait for the repetition. "No, I guess I never have," I replied.

"I meant with somebody inside it," Walter elaborated. The threat to my personal well-being was obvious.

The rest of the meeting was a series of ominous warnings: "You better take care of *our* people . . . You better respect *us* . . . You better treat *our* people right."

Throughout that summer and into the fall, I got to know Walter very well. Every day at one o'clock, he would storm into the office area full of secretaries and bellow, "Where's the f—ing idiot?" Some days he would change his insult to a vulgarity that referenced my mother and me.

Soon he was across from my desk, expounding on everything

I had done wrong in the past twenty-four hours. "You put out a work schedule yesterday and didn't discuss it first with the employees! Now Charles is upset about the shifts you gave him. What's the matter with you?"

The next day: "One of *our* people showed up a half hour late this morning, and the supervisor gave him a warning! How dare you reprimand him for such a little thing!"

The next day: "Your room manager's little motivation game for the housekeepers is insulting! You're treating us like little kids!"

I would try to explain my actions while including comments about the larger, overarching purpose of our operation. He wasn't buying it. Day after day, week after week, the tirades went on.

Then one day in October, Walter didn't show up. One fifteen passed . . . then one thirty . . . then one forty-five. I called my department supervisors and said, "Tell me anything— *anything*—bad that happened yesterday." They mentioned a couple of little things, but nothing major.

So I dashed out of my office and ran the eight blocks down to the union hall. I strode right in and demanded, "Where's Walter?"

"He's in a meeting," the receptionist said. "They're in executive session."

I started toward the conference room door.

"You can't go in there!"

I ignored the comment. Walking right into the room, I marched up to where Walter was sitting. "Where were you today?" I snapped. "We have business to do, and you didn't show up. At least you could have called me and apologized for missing our meeting!"

His face grew red. "You can't come in here!" he yelled.

"Look, I'm telling you, *show up* so we can do our work together for *your* members and *my* employees!" Then I walked out. I congratulated myself for upsetting their assumptions.

Later on, I was told that after I left the room, Walter said to his stewards with a grin, "That S.O.B. likes it!" None of them could quite figure out why their intimidation of me wasn't working.

Hot Coffee on a Cold Day

Relationships with the union were a little more balanced after that confrontation. But deep suspicions remained. The Christmas season drew near. Hyatt had a policy in those days that every employee was to receive a turkey for the holidays.

Walter and his union leaders were hardly grateful. "What the—? You're trying to bribe our members!" he ranted. Literally within minutes, a strike had been called. Employees were milling around outside the hotel chanting as they carried hastily made signs that read "Unfair to Labor."

And before heading out the door, they had pulled a little trick. They had punched a button on each cash register—at the front desk, the bar, the restaurant—that left the drawer standing open so any guest walking by could help themselves to money.

It happened to be a very cold winter day. I got my kitchen and restaurant supervisors together and said, "Quick, make some hot cider. Get together whatever sweet rolls and hot coffee you have. We're going to take them out to the strikers." I knew we had to hurry, because the TV cameras would show up soon; I knew they covered every strike in Pittsburgh.

By the time the news crews had arrived, my team and I were well underway, serving warm refreshments to the union members.

"What are you doing?" the confused TV reporter wanted to know, pushing a microphone toward my face.

"These are still our employees," I answered. "The fact that there's been a misunderstanding so that they're missing a little bit of work has nothing to do with the fact that they're a vital part of this hotel, and I love them. It's cold out here. I just thought they should have something hot to drink and sweet to eat."

You can imagine how well this played on the evening news.

Turnaround

From that time on, our meetings became more civil. Walter stopped calling me rude names, settling for simply "the German" or "the Kraut." Two years later, the union and I were getting along famously, and we had completely turned around the hotel's image.

We had disproven what a young PR agent had said at the end of an introductory meeting: "Horst, I need to tell you something, since you're new here in town. You can never make this into a great hotel." When I had asked him why not, he replied, "You don't get it, do you? You're here on the Hill. This is a black neighborhood. You can never overcome that fact." I promptly told him I would not be needing his services.

The day came when the city hosted a lunch for association executives—the auto dealers association, the education association, the health care association, and others. These were very important people to us, since they booked hotels for conferences and other events. The mayor was the featured speaker. He stood up and said, "What do we have to accomplish here in Pittsburgh? We have to adjust to new realities. We have to get creative. We need a rebirth of this city.

"I'm not just talking about our infrastructure. We won't have a renaissance by working only with buildings. We have to create a renaissance of the spirit. We have to do what has been done with the Hyatt hotel over on the Hill. It's been totally turned around. We have to get busy making this a city where everybody wants to come."

I could only sit there at my table and smile.

Not long afterward, the company transferred me to a Hyatt Regency in Dearborn, Michigan, a Detroit suburb. The last time I saw Jim the doorman, he brightened up and said, "Hello, Mr. Schulze!" We had met our shared objective of having the best hotel, the cleanest hotel, the friendliest hotel, committed to excellence, superior to our competition in every way—even with a union. In fact, the union was no longer an obstacle but instead an important factor in our success.

And it was especially gratifying to hear that Walter had called his local union president in Detroit to say, "The German is coming to your area. He's a good man. You'll be all right working with him."

In Search of Happiness

The relationship between leadership and labor is so much bigger than just wage scales and work rules. The Greek philosopher Aristotle taught us centuries ago, "The life of money-making is one undertaken under compulsion, and wealth is evidently not the good we are seeking; for it is merely useful and for the sake of something else."[1]

And what was that something else? Aristotle called it "happiness," which he took considerable pains to explain. To some people, he said it was merely *pleasure*; that was what they hoped to gain by making money. But to the more thoughtful, he said the goal was *honor*, the knowledge that they had done a quality job and that others admired them for doing so.

I believe this lies at the heart of every work relationship. Employees yearn for the happiness of fulfillment. Yes, they need a paycheck. But deeper than that, they want to be able to say they have done something excellent. They don't want to just grind through five (or six) days every week, being miserable so they can be happy on the weekend. They seek to combine happiness with earning a livelihood.

I'm not just talking about millennials. People sometimes criticize them for asking repeatedly, "What's in it for me?" This is nothing new. Older generations wanted to know the same objectives and motives as they do; we just didn't dare to ask. Millennials come right out with it, wanting to know what's the point.

If we as leaders do not give employees of all ages a dream worth joining, we get the labor strife we deserve.

PART THREE

BUILDING
TRUE LEADERSHIP

CHAPTER ELEVEN

LEADING IS AN ACQUIRED SKILL

How many times have you heard someone say about a successful quarterback (or governor or pastor or entrepreneur), "They're just a natural-born leader"?

A line from Shakespeare comes to mind. In the second act of *Twelfth Night*, the uptight antagonist Malvolio is handed a bogus letter supposedly from the woman he hopes to woo. There he reads, "Some are born great, some achieve greatness, and some have greatness thrust upon 'em. Thy fates open their hands, let thy blood and spirit embrace them."[1]

Is leadership primarily a matter of fate? Good DNA? Innate talent? Many people think so. A website called BC Technology boldly declared the following a number of years back:

> Leaders are born, not made. You either have it or you don't. The leadership gene should be mapped somewhere in the genome so we can develop a simple blood test early on and save tons of money and tons of anguish on those that try to lead, but fail miserably at it . . .
>
> Critical pieces of leadership are really core parts of your personality. You either have charisma or you don't. You were born with a love for hard work or you are lazy. You have self-confidence oozing from your pores or you have self-loathing.[2]

I beg to disagree. I have known too many leaders (including myself) who showed little aptitude in the early going for taking charge. They wouldn't have won a popularity contest or been voted most likely to succeed. They had neither "the look" nor the assumed requisite temperament of leadership.

Some strong leaders are indeed quite affable, but others are quietly deliberate. They don't talk much, but when they do, they're worth listening to. In other words, leaders do not all possess one personality. Take, for example, the apostles Jesus chose, who ranged from obstreperous Peter to cautious Thomas. Jesus chose both "work the system" Matthew (a tax collector for the Romans) and firebrand protestor Simon the Zealot.

As Susan Cain writes in her national bestseller *Quiet*, "Contrary to the model . . . of vocal leadership, the ranks of effective CEOs turn out to be filled with introverts, including Charles Schwab; Bill Gates; Brenda Barnes, CEO of Sara Lee; and James Copeland, former CEO of Deloitte Touche Tohmatsu."[3]

Everybody, whatever their bent, can muster the inner fortitude to first lead *themselves* before trying to lead others. What does this entail? It means focusing on the future, setting a worthy objective that will be good for all concerned, and then figuring out how to communicate this to employees and other stakeholders.

In this way, leaders develop themselves over time. They don't rely on magic from a black box. They discipline themselves to discern a clear vision and then set about pursuing it. Granted, they don't get everything right the first time, but they learn from their misjudgments and figure out how to be more effective in the next round.

I sometimes get the chance to speak at college commencements. I say something like this to the excited graduates in robes and mortarboards seated before me:

Today you cannot help feeling that you have achieved. You have earned a degree. But close your eyes for a moment and ask yourself where you want to be in five years. Do you have a real plan? Do you have a vision that is beautiful? Does it hold value? Or are you just going to head out into the world and see what happens? If you want to become an electrical engineer, for example, how are you going to get there? Do you need to go to graduate school or not? What are the steps that will get you to your goal? When you arrive twenty years down the road and look back on your life, what will you see? Will you be proud of your record, or will you see only a fog of meandering?

Of course, I get a round of applause at the end. Some graduates even come up to me afterward and say, "Great speech!" At one university, somebody actually turned my comments into a rap song and posted it on YouTube.

My point is, leaders are dreamers. They set their sights on worthwhile goals that will be good not only for themselves but also for their families, their colleagues, their employees, their customers, their investors, and society at large. If they aspire only to chase after personal fame or fortune, life will probably knock them down. But if they set out to make a specific contribution to the world, they can go far.

Visions Require Decisions

Once the vision is in place, the practical work begins—the work of making conscious decisions about how to bring that vision to pass.

For example, if I say, "I envision a great marriage, so I have decided to love my wife," I need to be aware of what that entails. It means I will take notice of her needs and wishes. I will protect her as best I can from dangers, be they physical or financial. I will participate with her in the arduous work of raising children together. I will compliment her achievements, both in the home and beyond. This list could go on and on—the implications of my decision to love her.

Now if I say I envision building a strong furniture chain or a leading taxi service or an effective mission to serve the poor, I have to decide some things. Leadership is a lot about conscious decision making. It is about making up your mind that certain things *are* going to happen, because you're going to pursue them relentlessly. You're going to let nothing stand in your way.

Here are four decisions I've made that have helped me bring my vision to pass. You can adapt them to your situation.

Decision Number One: Strive to Inspire

Because employees are important, I will create an environment where people *want* to do a good job. I will invite, not dictate. I will get results by inspiring, not by controlling or mandating. When you are the boss, the trappings of hierarchy can tempt you into thinking you can order people around. You hold the power—and it feels good, doesn't it? If they don't do what you want, you can fire them. It's your show to run, after all.

Yes, those things are true. But having this mind-set won't get you the best outcomes. When employees sense that you don't really trust them, that you're mainly watching, eagle-eyed, for their next mistake, productivity goes into a slide. All sense of momentum is lost.

The organization you want is the one with energy and initiative, even joy. This comes about because the leader has fostered a healthy climate that inspires others to pursue excellence. You will actually have more power if people want to follow you than if they run away from you.

But at the same time, there's another decision to make . . .

Decision Number Two: Don't Settle for Less

I won't settle for less than the vision. No excuses allowed, either from myself or those who work with me. As I said previously, there is no beauty in the excuse or "explanation." No forward motion comes from it.

One winter, I noticed that our Boston hotel's January occupancy rate was down to 55 percent. We had budgeted for 68 percent. I phoned the general manager there.

"What happened?" I asked. "How come we did only 55 percent last month?"

"Well, you know, we had a terrible blizzard. Snow and ice everywhere—it was awful." He was no longer thinking about the objective; he was comfortable in the explanation.

"Well, frankly," I replied, "I didn't call for the weather report. Let me ask you this: What was the occupancy rate at the Copley Plaza [our main downtown competitor in the luxury market]?"

"Well, they were very slow too," the manager said.

"So, I guess that implies they had at least *some* rooms occupied," I said. "I want to know why those guests didn't come to us instead. You can't tell me they got off the plane at Logan Airport and said to themselves, 'Because of the blizzard I think I'll go to Copley Plaza.'

"Here's the thing: If you're comfortable with a low rate

this year, we'll have a problem next year too. It's going to snow hard again next winter. The question is, what are you going to *do* about it? I say get busy promoting your location; tell people, 'This is your opportunity to experience luxury at a discount!'"

I also told him to get busy analyzing which companies and organizations held their annual meetings in Boston during that season and then to quickly court their business for the following year. We offered them a discount price if they would prepay. As a result, we ended up stealing contracts from other hotels!

I don't pay people to think up "explanations"; I pay them to find answers. In the weeks following 9/11, I found that some hotel managers were relieved that they didn't have to figure out why occupancy rates were so low. Now they had the ideal excuse: *Nobody's traveling; business is down all over.* But that's not the correct mind-set.

If anybody had an excuse for poor business, it would have been stores in Houston when Hurricane Harvey slammed ashore in August 2017, with winds up to 130 miles per hour and as much as 60 inches of rain in America's fourth-largest city. Employees were flooded out; roads became impassable; electricity failed; and dozens of people drowned.

But that didn't stop one grocery chain, H-E-B, from serving its customers. Within thirty-six hours of the hurricane's landfall, sixty of its eighty-three stores across the Houston area were open again. Scott McClelland, president of the Houston division, tells of some of the extraordinary steps he and his team took in those awful days and nights: "We first knew the storm was coming last Tuesday [four days ahead, so] . . . we began shipping [bottled] water and bread into the affected areas. Those are the two categories people buy first. When you go into a hurricane, nobody buys frozen food. You want milk, bread, water. You want batteries, you want canned meat. You want tuna."

Many of the H-E-B truck drivers were stuck in their homes or had lost them altogether. So McClelland used helicopters to fly drivers in from San Antonio, the corporate headquarters. "The neck in the funnel, really in our capacity," said McClelland, "was to get enough drivers to be able to get our trucks out of the yard and get them delivered." (On one day, though, they had to suspend flights because President Trump was coming, and the airspace was closed.)

McClelland said they called Proctor & Gamble and Kimberly-Clark and told them to send entire trailer loads of toilet paper and paper towels directly to the stores. "One store will take half a trailer," said McClelland, "and the other store will take the other half. You can just bypass our warehouse, so you can get it to us [quicker]. In doing that, I create more capacity in my distribution chain. So, you send direct trucks—here are the stores you can go to—and split the truck: make it half paper towels and half toilet tissue."

McClelland also told the interviewer, "I called Frito-Lay and said . . . I need Lay's, I need Doritos, I need Fritos. I need a variety pack. I don't need Funyons and I don't need Munchos. Just make your best sellers. I won't turn down any delivery. We'll take it as fast as we can."

The company atmosphere was such that employees from outside the region began volunteering to come help. They would spend up to eighteen hours cleaning up a store and restocking it, and then they'd go sleep on somebody's couch until the next sunrise.

After five days, McClelland reported, "Sales are down [only] 4 percent versus a year ago. And that's with a number of stores not being open at all some days. I'll take that. I'll end the week with sales up from a year ago; frankly, sales are the least of my worries.

"I do the commercials for H-E-B in Houston, so people know who I am. So, as I walked in the store, people would come up and hug me and thank us for making the effort to open because the Kroger across the street wasn't open. The Walmart down the street wasn't open. One woman walked up and started crying and she hugged me to thank us for being open."[4]

Sounds to me like a man and a company centered on the vision of serving, not making excuses for what "can't be done."

Decision Number Three: Let Nothing Cloud Your Vision

I will not let my company's growth and complexity cloud my vision. The bigger an organization becomes, the more complex it becomes, the more people you hire, the more departments you set up—and as all this evolves, the easier it is to neglect the vision. Something negative happens on any given day, and managers write a policy to keep that from happening again. The next month, something else happens, and another policy gets written. Soon the policy manual is four hundred pages thick.

This is what is called a bureaucracy. People are afraid to get outside of the rules and regulations. Growth is stunted. So is creativity.

We could all tell stories about companies that used to be nimble and energetic in pursuit of their vision, but over the decades they've grown fat and sluggish. The reason to come to work has migrated away from building a great organization toward protecting one's turf, not getting in trouble, and avoiding disruptions.

In contrast to this, let me offer one more decision that a leader needs to make.

INNOVATION IS OFTEN *SQUELCHED* IN THE NAME OF TRADITION

Decision Number Four: Always Look to Improve

I will always keep looking for new ways to improve, to be more efficient. True leaders never stop asking, "How can we improve this process? Who should I ask to help me think of a better approach? And am I willing to hear things that don't fit my preconceptions?" As Albert Einstein is reported to have said, "If at first the idea is not absurd, then there is no hope for it."[5]

I learned long ago in the hotel business to pull together a staff the day after the Thanksgiving weekend and say, "All right, what did customers say? What could we have done better? What should we adjust for next year?" Everybody had an opportunity to say their piece. This was more than just a gabfest; we wrote down the feedback into a plan that had to be finished by December 15. After the Christmas/New Year's rush, we would repeat the exercise.

The old phrase "we've never done it that way before" has no place in a healthy organization. Innovation is often squelched in the name of tradition. When defects reveal themselves, we need to talk about it. We need to keep telling each other that we can do better next time around.

Are You Actually a Leader?

Leadership implies that somebody has a destination in view and is taking people along to that destination. Managers don't do that; they only manage processes and force things to happen. Leaders, on the other hand, seek to create an environment where people want to do the things needed to reach the destination.

At one point in my career, I was responsible for sixty-five local hotels. I sat down one day, scrutinized each of them, and came to the conclusion that I had five leaders and sixty managers! What a wake-up call.

How did I determine this? Well, I had asked each of the individuals, "So, what will this hotel be next year?" In too many cases, I heard, "Well, if I had a bigger ballroom . . . if we could do a remodel . . . if the labor force in this city had a better work ethic . . ." Excuses, excuses. I actually heard one or two of them say their operation could be termed a "strong average." What? That would be the bottom of "good" and the top of "bad."

From the five leaders, however, I heard things such as, "In another year, everybody in this community is going to love this hotel! It's going to be really exciting." They were headed for a beautiful future, and if along the way they happened to fall down in some mud puddle, they were determined to pop right back up and focus on the horizon again. They would lead themselves and their people toward the goal.

This graphic summarizes the main points I've made in this chapter.

- It starts at the top with *understanding the vision*: What is the vision of this organization? What does it expect of me?
- Next comes *making a conscious decision to achieve that vision*. But you don't keep this a secret inside yourself. You *clearly communicate* this to everyone on your team.
- Then it's time to get to work *executing the plan*, figuring out the actionable steps that align with the vision, and not allowing yourself to get sidetracked by other distractions.
- The fourth part is *maintaining focus* at all times. No excuses or rationalizations.

LEADERSHIP IS . . .

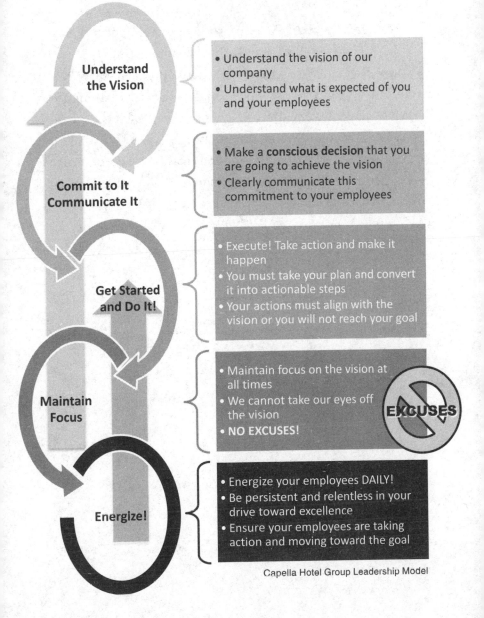

Understand the Vision
- Understand the vision of our company
- Understand what is expected of you and your employees

Commit to It Communicate It
- Make a **conscious decision** that you are going to achieve the vision
- Clearly communicate this commitment to your employees

Get Started and Do It!
- Execute! Take action and make it happen
- You must take your plan and convert it into actionable steps
- Your actions must align with the vision or you will not reach your goal

Maintain Focus
- Maintain focus on the vision at all times
- We cannot take our eyes off the vision
- **NO EXCUSES!**

Energize!
- Energize your employees DAILY!
- Be persistent and relentless in your drive toward excellence
- Ensure your employees are taking action and moving toward the goal

Capella Hotel Group Leadership Model

- And finally comes *energizing employees* to join you in your persistent drive toward excellence.

Does this sound like a lot of work? It is! You probably were not born knowing how to pull this off automatically. Maybe your teachers and coaches back in school didn't call you a "natural leader." But if you set your mind to the task, making the crucial decisions we've discussed above, you'll achieve success. You'll find that you *can* lead quite naturally.

As you see your vision come into reality, it will be worth every ounce of effort you have put forth. You've made yourself into a leader, and your leadership is paying off.

CHAPTER TWELVE

WHY VISION STATEMENTS MATTER

Results-oriented leaders sometimes get bored with incessant talk about vision and mission. They're wary of cute little slogans. They've sat through enough group marathons trying to forge a sentence or paragraph that will please everyone, tweaking this word and that phrase, blah blah blah, to the point of exhaustion. *Can't we just get out of here and return to work?*

Besides, what difference does a vision statement really make in the real world? Aren't they all like the every-fourth-year platform of the Republican Party or the Democratic Party—a grandiose jumble of ideas and wishes that few people even read or listen to, because they know the platform will be forgotten a few days after the nominating convention ends? It's just a bunch of words.

If an organizational proclamation is no more than a pile of frothy rhetoric to put in the annual report, then, yes, it's pointless. In fact, it can breed cynicism in both the employees and the public. One of the major airlines experienced this not long ago when its treatment of passengers didn't quite match up to "fly the friendly skies."

What's the Destination?

If taken seriously, a vision statement can serve as a company's North Star, pointing in the direction it intends to go. If you get into your car and just start driving without a destination in mind, you may end up somewhere you don't like. If, however, you choose a destination ahead of time, knowing it's a place you'll really enjoy, you will head out with anticipation. It's going to be worth your time and gasoline to get there.

Once you say, "I'm going *there*," everything else falls into place. You put the key in the ignition, pull up a map (on paper or on your phone), and begin the purposeful journey.

The same thing proves valuable in an organization. You set a destination, often with the counsel of your colleagues. You then align your actions. You show your employees how you're all going to get there together. You give them a purpose to get out of bed in the morning and come to work. And together you start moving forward.

When I first proposed, back in my Hyatt days, that we adopt a company-wide model of "Ladies and Gentlemen Serving Ladies and Gentlemen" (from my earliest days in the Kurhaus back in Germany), I wasn't taken seriously. Some took it as a joke. I didn't have enough seniority to press the issue, but I could at least start instilling it into the one hotel I was managing at the time.

I didn't send out a memo or print up posters; I just talked with my employees. "Look," I said to them, "you're not lowly servants. You are ladies and gentlemen who serve the guests. You can be professional about this! If you sentence yourself to be just a servant, then that means you're not a professional. But you can be higher than a servant.

"And the people coming through our front door—they're not jerks. They're not just a credit card to us. They, too, are ladies and gentlemen, and they're paying to be treated as such.

Otherwise, they could go to a cheap hotel or motel down the street. But we respect them for who they truly are."

Nine years later, when I was asked to create the Ritz-Carlton model, I had the standing to install this viewpoint on Day One. "We respect everyone who walks in as a lady or a gentleman. And we will respect every employee in the same way, behaving accordingly."

Someone said to me, "Well, not every guest acts like a lady or a gentleman. Some of them can be very obnoxious."

"Yes, I know," I replied, "but it's not up to us to judge or categorize. They may have made their decision to be cantankerous, but we've made our decision to respect them regardless. This is our value; this is our identity. It's who we are, regardless."

I truly believe this is one of the key reasons that we became the number one hotel brand in the world throughout the 1990s.

More Than Words

Slogans and vision statements on the wall don't work. *Belief systems* work. *Culture* works. The slogan or statement must be simply an interpretation of the real meaning and life within an organization. At the core, you have decided to be a certain kind of operation. It is in your DNA. And you need to distill that essence into a set of words.

You have to remind yourself and others of these words constantly. They have to be alive inside your soul. You don't mind repeating them again and again—at the start of meetings, in casual conversations on the shop floor, in the office, in the break room—because they're so important. You say it because you and your people are *living it*.

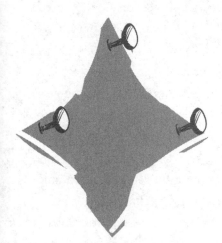

SLOGANS *and* VISION STATEMENTS ON A WALL DON'T WORK

BELIEF SYSTEMS WORK

CULTURE WORKS

When a particular employee isn't living it, isn't doing what they said they were willing to do back at the beginning, and is perhaps even working *against* the vision, you may be tempted to ask, "What happened? I thought Bill was fully on board here. But it's certainly not looking that way now."

Maybe the person has undergone a change of heart or has a life circumstance they haven't talked about. But maybe you as a leader haven't kept the vision constantly in front of them. Before you blame them for underperformance, first check your own performance in reinforcing the vision.

And besides, the constant repetition holds *you* accountable to yourself. Every time I verbalize the Capella Hotel Group's commitment to "fulfill individual customer expectations," I have to ask myself, *Are we still doing that? Is that actually happening this week?* When I say the phrase about having "respected and empowered employees who work in an environment of belonging and purpose," it brings me face-to-face with how the workplace environment is actually doing these days. Is it healthy, or is it deteriorating—and if it is deteriorating, what should I be doing differently?

In Rough Waters

Vision statements hold you steady when times get tough. They set the tone when the market goes turbulent or when you must make a hard call about someone's continued employment. Your emotions may be pulling you to one side (fear) or another (loyalty to your friend). But the vision statement stands immovable: *This is who we are. This is our culture. And therefore, I must do . . .*

Leaders sometimes complain, "Oh, making decisions is so hard." Most of the time, however, it's not—as long as the purpose of the organization is clearly stated. You set objectives that you know are good for all concerned, and then you force yourself to follow through in alignment with that vision.

Yes, it can sometimes be painful to do so. You may endure some sleepless nights. You worry about the ripple effects on people's careers, their spouses, and their children. But you know what the vision statement calls you to do. And once you make the commitment to stay true to your vision statement, a lot of secondary decisions start lining up with clarity.

I once served on the board of an organization that would start every board meeting by plunging immediately into the quarterly numbers and other details of the operation. All the reports were ready and waiting on the big table when we walked in. After a few meetings, I got to the point of saying, "Wait a minute. We should first read the vision and values of this company. There's no point plowing through all these reports unless we're focused on accomplishing the vision."

The group agreed. From that day forward, every board meeting began with the reading of the corporate vision out loud. It set the stage for the discussions to follow.

On another board where I serve, the Cancer Treatment Centers of America, this focus is taken even further. Every board meeting includes a *live report* from one of our actual patients, plus their spouse or other caretaker, on how we are doing from their perspective, how their treatment is going, what we're doing well, what we could be doing better. We even fly the patient in from another city if necessary. This keeps us zeroed in on what our mission is all about. Our chairman is famous for asking repeatedly, "What can we do better? I appreciate all the compliments, but we can't learn from those. I want to know what we can do to improve."

The very reason for a board meeting—or any meeting actually—is to focus on the vision and accomplish the mission. The vision is a constant reminder of the direction we have said we're going to head. We dare not wander away from that.

CHAPTER THIRTEEN

A LEADER'S "GUT" IS NOT ENOUGH

Heads of organizations are sometimes impatient about taking formal performance measurements, especially if the research is expensive. Their explanations are well-known and often heard:

- "We're awfully busy this year. Maybe next year."
- "It will cost too much money."
- "Those research firms just try to milk you for every extra dollar they can."
- "How do I know the results won't be biased?"
- "The P&L statement tells the tale well enough."

To me, trying to lead an organization without taking measurements is like trying to coach a football game without yard markers. How would you ever know how close you were to a first down? How could you ever decide whether to kick a field goal? You would simply be guessing.

It is absolutely essential to know where a company stands. Measurement is how we determine the gap between where we think we are and where we actually are. Have I set a goal to grow my operation? Have I decided I'm going to be superior to the competition? Have I set out to be "the best" in my field? If I don't measure things, I won't know which gaps need to be filled, and that means I won't know where I need to improve.

Some people think measurement is the boss's tool for control—a game of "gotcha," a scheme to make employees look bad. No, that's not the point at all. There is a difference between *inspection* and *measurement.* Inspection means you're looking over someone's shoulder, trying to catch them messing up. Measurement means taking samples to determine if you and the people you've chosen for your organization are fulfilling your overall vision—and if not, how to get closer to the goal in the future.

A Leader's Intuition Is Not Enough

Entrepreneurs are famous for working by their feelings. That's usually how they got their start. They just had an instinct for what could succeed—a product or service that was missing in the marketplace but would draw people's attention.

So far, so good. *Time* magazine once ran a feature on "The Man with the Golden Gut"—the legendary television producer Fred Silverman, who launched everything from *Scooby-Doo* to *All in the Family* to *The Waltons* to the miniseries *Roots*.[1] We all admire visionaries who seem to have a knack for coming up with great hits in their field.

But where do things stand *today*? Is their original genius still producing the results it once did? Will it continue to do so in the future? The entrepreneur's hunch or "gut" is not enough to tell.

Financial Stats Are Not Enough

The corporate after-tax earnings figures are certainly important and deserving of every leader's close attention. These numbers are closely watched by stakeholders on all sides, from the governing board to (in some cases) Wall Street. They tell the difference between black ink and red ink.

But by themselves, statistics are only a snapshot of one quarter or one year. And by the time the numbers are crunched and published, they're already at least six weeks out of date. The profit and loss numbers don't indicate at all what you will be tomorrow or next year. They don't help you steer a future course. In this, they are seriously incomplete.

Hard Work Is Not Enough

When I opened the first Ritz-Carlton in Atlanta, I had a dream, a feel, for what this hotel should be. I put in long hours from early in the morning until well into the evening. Some days I would come home for dinner with my wife and young daughters and then go back to the hotel and keep working until ten or even up to midnight. I was exhausted—especially when I would wake up again at three or four in the morning thinking about yet another issue that needed my attention.

We soon opened a second hotel in Atlanta. I kept pushing hard, making sure every detail was handled correctly. But then the third hotel in the chain was slated to open in California. Now what? I couldn't rely on my personal oversight to make it successful. How would I know what was really going on two thousand miles west?

I had to start measuring.

"Luck" and "Hope" Will Never Be Enough

Getting "lucky" is not a strategy. Neither is just "hoping for the best." We all appreciate those times when we get a break out of nowhere, and the wind seems to be at our back for a season. But we also know this doesn't happen with any predictability. We have to lead through the difficult times as well as the easy ones.

Anything that is important in an operation has to be measured. I mentioned briefly in chapter 10 about the New York City hotel that was suffering low satisfaction rates among both customers and employees and how it dramatically improved in just two years. How did this happen?

I actually moved into that hotel for three months, traveling back home to my family on the weekends. One thing I noticed quickly was that as I approached the concierge desk, the person didn't look at me; his eyes were fixed on the computer screen in front of him. Emails were taking precedence over people. I said to myself that I'd rather have no concierge desk at all than one that ignored guests who wanted to ask a question.

I found out that this staff was not having any kind of daily communication, such as a lineup meeting at the beginning of a shift. They had long forgotten the main point of being in business—to serve the customer. They were too busy—you might even say, "New York busy."

I started meeting with the doormen, the bellmen, and the maids. I sat down with each department head—from food service to purchasing. I remember asking the housekeeping manager, "Okay, on a scale of one to ten, how do you see your department?"

He thought for a moment and then boldly said, "Ten."

"That's very interesting. Let's go and have a look at some rooms."

He got his pass key, and we started down the corridors, checking out a half dozen or so rooms and taking note of how clean they were. I pointed out various defects all along the way. Then we returned to my office.

"Now one more time," I said, "how would you rate your department?"

In a sheepish voice he replied, "I guess about a six."

"You see," I said then, "a ten is very difficult to achieve. Now that we have a baseline of six, tell me this: When will you move it up to a ten? And what do you need from me to reach that level? I'm not here to beat you up; I'm here to help you. Let me come to each meeting with your employees to encourage them. I will thank them for what they're doing. And I'll tell them that they define themselves as human beings by the job they're doing."

He and I set up a plan for him to report back to me every month with where things stood: Seven? Eight? Nine? The upsurge was dramatic.

I did much the same with the other department heads. Within one year, the numbers across the establishment were soaring. Both *U.S. News & World Report* and the online travel site TripAdvisor rated us the best hotel in New York.

I was at an early-morning Bible study one day attended by a lot of Wall Street brokers, and a fellow said to me, "So where is your hotel?"

"On Fifth Avenue between Thirty-Sixth and Thirty-Seventh Streets," I answered.

"Oh, that's the one with the nice doormen!" he volunteered.

The culture was entirely different from before, as employees had aligned themselves with the vision of being the best, the friendliest, the most welcoming. They had wanted to do a good job; they just hadn't realized what that entailed.

What to Measure

Now we come to the biggest question of all: *What should a leader measure?*

I say that it should be no more than four or five important things. Otherwise, you can get bogged down in hundreds of secondary items, from the frequency of window cleaning to the price of paper clips. You will be swimming in statistics to the point where you don't know which end is up.

Here are "the Big Three" as far as I'm concerned. You may want to add one or two of your own, as long as they are significant benchmarks.

1. **Customer satisfaction/loyalty.** You can't guess at this; you have to *ask* them through regular surveys (paper or online) what they're thinking. The most telling questions are these: "How likely are you to come back again?" and "How likely are you to recommend us to your friends?"

    Any summary rating under a 90 percent top line is a red flag to me. I want to know why they don't think they'll return to do business with me. Was it our fault? Was it something we can correct? All my hotel managers knew that any slippage below the top two boxes (a nine or a ten) would trigger my direct involvement. I would be calling to say, "So now, what are we going to do about this? How are we going to get back up above 90 percent next month? What is it going to take?"

2. **Employee satisfaction.** Just as vital to the health of an organization is what the people who work there think of their environment. Again, you can't assume everybody is

a happy camper except for one or two complainers. You must *ask* for their assessment on a recurring schedule. If you just go by what you happen to hear, you will be misled. Formal measurement tells you what is really on their minds. If eight employees say they're short of equipment, that's significant. If just one employee says it, you can lay it aside until more evidence arises.

After many years of analysis, I can state with confidence that a drop of just 1 percent on the employee satisfaction survey translates into a perceptible impact on the company's bottom line. It means, among other things, that employee turnover is going to rise. More job knowledge is going to be walking out the door, and to replace that knowledge is going to push up costs.

Employee satisfaction assessments tell a leader what is going on, and they show what responses need to be made to stay healthy as an organization.

3. **Leading indicators.** This third vital measurement looks to the future. It wants to know how the landscape is going to be six months or a year down the road. Are people coming our way for service at the same rate as they always have, or are they slacking off? Is the customer population getting older, younger, or staying the same? Are they spending the same as they always have, or less?

For example, in the hotel business we look at advance bookings. What percentage of our rooms are already booked for, say, the coming January or April or October compared to a year ago? Two years ago? These numbers tell us how well we're doing at keeping customers and getting new ones.

A leader must also look at what the overall economy is doing. I remember taking notice back in 1980 that a recession was coming. Layoffs were increasing; inflation was in the 12 to 13 percent range; and the Federal Reserve kept trying to fight it by raising interest rates. The state of Michigan, where I was running the Dearborn Hyatt at the time, would end up leading the nation with 14.5 percent unemployment by the fall of 1982.

I called a general meeting of the entire staff—department managers, cooks, front-desk people, right down to the newest busboys. "Okay, everybody," I said, "we're going to have a recession next year. Don't ask me how I know; I just do. I'm sure of it. Yes, we have a good batch of group reservations already on the books—conferences and all that. But they can pull out at any time. We have to keep every customer we can.

"What happens in a recession? We have five restaurants in this hotel. Let's say a couple normally goes out to eat four times a month. Now during a recession, they won't stop altogether; they will keep going out, but maybe only three times a month. That's a 25 percent drop!

"Every one of us in this room has to move heaven and earth to keep every customer now. Otherwise, you won't have a job by this time next year. It's that serious."

As I left the room that day, I walked past a cluster of bellmen and doormen talking in low tones with one another. When they spotted me, they paused. Something seemed odd. They all happened to be African Americans, and in my mind I began to speculate. *They're talking negatively about me, the white boss. They're saying I'm just trying to get more work out of them.*

The recession of the early '80s hit the economy hard. But we managed to stay afloat; in fact, we had a great year, while others suffered through layoffs. Why? Because we were doing everything we could to keep guests liking us.

In time, I moved on to another assignment. It was twenty-five years before I got back to Dearborn. Lo and behold, two of the bellmen still worked there and recognized me. "Oh, Mr. Schulze, it's good to see you again!" they exclaimed. "We will never forget what you did during that recession year. In fact, a group of us got together right at the end of that meeting and discussed what we could do to keep customers happy."

In that moment, I felt so rebuked for having misjudged their intent so long ago. "I'm glad for what you and the others did back then! We got through it, didn't we?" I said. And then I called my wife to say, "Remember Dearborn? You won't believe who I ran into today!"

Paying attention to leading indicators and making quick responses had saved all our lives.

Shooting for the Stars

By the time I had moved to the Ritz-Carlton start-up project, a measurement program had come along that had risen above all others: the Malcolm Baldrige National Quality Award. This was no small gimmick; it was a federal government initiative to recognize United States companies doing top-quality management. The award is named after the late Malcolm Baldrige Jr., long-serving secretary of commerce during the Reagan administration. Awards were given each year in six categories—manufacturing, service, small business, education, health care, and nonprofit. The goal was to hold up exemplary models for others to follow in order to make American companies more competitive with their foreign counterparts.

Well, if I was going to create the best hotel company in the world, I should be able to win in the service category, right? We had won a few other awards along the way—among them, the Pinnacle Award from *Successful Meetings* magazine and a nice honor from *Travel + Leisure* magazine. In fact, one of the meeting planner groups had voted us the best hotel chain in America. So we executives got together one evening for a fancy dinner and high-fived each other, feeling very good about ourselves.

The only trouble was, the next morning I opened my mail and got hit with a flurry of complaints from guests who had heard about the vote and didn't think Ritz-Carlton was all that great. It brought me down a peg or two from the night before.

I had lunch that day with an older gentleman named Roger Milliken, the chairman and CEO of a textile manufacturer that had won the Baldrige Award in 1989 in the manufacturing category. "Congratulations, Horst," he said. "You have the finest hotel chain in America!"

"Well, I read my mail this morning," I replied, "and if we are the best, we're the best of a lousy lot." I went on to tell him what had happened.

"Maybe you should check into the Baldrige Award criteria," he said at last. He described how thorough the program was and gave me a contact name in Washington.

I followed through, and soon thereafter, I was given a half-hour appointment, from 11:30 to noon, with the chief of criteria at the Department of Commerce. He explained how they dig into each applicant's operations, interview personnel at all levels, and rate both strengths and weaknesses. My head was swimming with information.

As noon approached, the man said, "Do you have time for lunch?" He told me years later that he made this offer because he could tell I hadn't understood a word he was saying, and he was feeling sorry for me!

I nodded. And so he took me to lunch, where he kept bombarding me with input. Some points made sense to me, but others flew right over my head.

"How do you make sure your rooms are clean?" he asked me at one point.

"Oh, I have a system for that," I answered a bit cockily. "For every four maids, there's an inspector who checks on their work. And for every inspector, we have an assistant manager who inspects one or two."

The man interrupted. "What if you didn't have to inspect them all?"

"Well, that would be great. It would save a lot of money. But we have to be sure."

He brought up an analogy. "If you inspect your swimming pool for purity, do you take out all the water for inspection or just a sample?"

"Just a sample," I answered.

"My point is, if your processes are right, you don't have to check *everything*. It's a matter of getting the processes aligned with the results you want."

By the time I left Washington that day, I knew I had a lot to learn about achieving real quality. But I was excited to try. For the next two years, I read Baldrige material, listened to speeches, and went to visit finalists and winners of the award, such as USAA (an insurance and financial services company), Graniterock (a quarry in California), and Zytec (a computer manufacturer in Minnesota). Up to that point, nobody had won in the service category except FedEx.

I then rolled out my dream at a meeting of Ritz-Carlton general managers, translating some of the complicated jargon into simpler words. "Here are the criteria for a truly fine company," I said, giving the list:

- leadership
- strategic planning
- customer and market focus
- measurement, analysis, and knowledge management
- human resource focus
- process management
- business results[2]

"It's not guesswork; it's not subjective opinion," I said. "These people will examine every corner of what we do to see if we know what customers want and are set up to provide it. Let's find out."

To make a long story short, it was a very difficult implementation. For just one example, we had to build a library of facts to support our claims of customer satisfaction, as well as show how they compared to our industry at large. Before the application was completely processed, the Baldrige people had gone out to interview employees in every one of our hotels—some two thousand individuals altogether.

And we didn't win the award.

But we wouldn't give up. We were learning so much about the science of measurement. We kept at it. Success finally came in 1992, when we were one of just five companies honored. We were so much better for all the effort we had invested.

We hadn't done this for fame and glory, although I will admit it was nice to go to the ceremony and receive the award from the president of the United States. We had done this to learn things we would have never discovered otherwise. Now we were obligated by Baldrige rules to open our doors and share with other companies what we had learned. Some famous names—Disney, for example—asked to interview us and find out what we had gained.

Once you win a Baldrige Award, you're not allowed to try again for five years. When that time had passed, I said to my team, "Let's go for a second award. It's never been done in our category, but why not us?"

My number one vice president came to me and said, "Horst, I've worked for you for many years, all the way back to our Hyatt days. You've always pushed hard, but this time, you're out of line. We're growing. We're opening new hotels. We have so much to do. We're going international now, and you want to apply for another Baldrige? This is too much. You're being unreasonable."

I replied, "I hear you, Eddie. In fact, I agree with you. But let me ask you, If we apply again, would we all have to study and learn more?"

"Yes."

RESULTS DON'T COME
FROM HIDING OURSELVES...

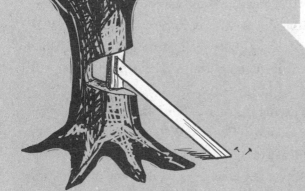

...FROM REALITY

RESULTS EMERGE AS WE MEASURE OUR REALITIES
AND MAKE ADJUSTMENTS

"Consequently, will the company be a little better?"

"Yes."

"Will that be good for the investors?"

"Yes."

"Will it be good for the employees?"

"Yes."

"Will it be good for all concerned?"

"Yes. Okay, let's do it."

We plunged back into the Baldrige swirl. And in 1999, we won a second award.

Yes, it cost us money. We could have said, "It's too expensive. We'll just keep doing the best we can on our own." But that would have been like someone saying, "Yes, I have cancer, but that surgery is too expensive. Plus, the radiation and chemotherapy will cost even more. I can't afford it."

Well, do you want to stay alive, or not?

Organizations that measure—and keep on measuring—find out their shortcomings. They discover strategies and tactics that need to be changed. They "take their medicine" and do what must be done for their ongoing health. That's part of the pain of business.

There's an old saying that goes, "You can't expect what you don't inspect." My version of that is this: "You won't accomplish what you don't measure." Results don't come from hiding ourselves from reality. They emerge as we measure our realities and make adjustments, and then measure again and keep adjusting. No matter how good you are, you keep looking for hidden defects, and you keep moving a little closer to true excellence.

The commitment to measuring and adjusting is not a luxury. It is essential to responsible leadership.

CHAPTER FOURTEEN

MONEY AND LOVE

Do *What You Love, the Money Will Follow* was the title of a hot book back in the late 1980s and early '90s that made bestseller lists and ended up selling more than a million copies. Written by a Los Angeles schoolteacher who left the education field to become a successful business psychologist, the book promised help in, as the subtitle says, *Discovering Your Right Livelihood.*[1]

As you can tell, the focus was mainly inward. Chapter titles included the following:

- "The Belief System Called 'Myself'"
- "Expressing Your Distinctive Self"
- "Treating Yourself as if You Count"

Well, yes, it is a good thing to love your field of work. I certainly have loved the hospitality arena ever since I was young. It gets me up and running in the morning.

When at one point I worked in a corporate office, there was a reserved parking place for me in the garage right next to the elevator. I never used it. I always parked at the hotel next door so I could walk through the lobby . . . say hello to the doorman . . . watch the guests checking out in the morning . . . swing through the pastry shop for a (not at all necessary) sweet roll . . . and eventually go to the office tower next door. It just gave me a warm feeling to sense the vibrations of a busy hotel.

But the more accurate truth is this: Do what the *customer* loves, and the money will follow.

That is how your paycheck gets generated. That is what makes an organization stay alive and thrive. If the public likes what you're providing and the way you're providing it, they'll be willing to pay you for it.

If a person focuses only on doing what they personally love—say, playing video games on the couch all day or writing obscure poetry that even their mother can't understand—the money will not follow. Passion has to align with the real world in some dimension. Not that there's anything wrong with video games or esoteric poems; anyone is free to pursue them on their own time. But in order to do something productive, an individual absolutely has to get in sync with real living, breathing human beings.

We all must be careful not to be driven by our personal desires. Not everybody thinks like you or I think. We are just a "sampling of one"—which is not enough to float a business. The customers (constituents, members, donors, or whatever name you use) have their own set of desires, for which they are willing to spend money. When we recognize those desires and set about to meet them, the wheels of a viable business begin to turn.

Eight Key Questions

The work of connecting with what customers love has a number of steps to it, which I've been outlining throughout this book. If I have the chance to speak to a class of aspiring hotel students and have been given only fifty minutes, here is how I march them through the sequence.

1. Make a decision about *what industry* you're going to enter. Is it truly going to be hotels? Then don't get side-tracked into other endeavors.

2. Decide which *market segment* of this industry you're going to pursue. The "budget" or "bargain" end of the spectrum? The midrange? The top end (which is what I chose)? There's nothing wrong with any of these. But you have to be clear about which one is yours.

3. Zero in on *what customers want* in this market segment. Who is willing to spend the kind of money you're going to charge? And what all do they expect in return? Don't assume you already know; you'll have to *ask* them. What are they truly looking for, even if they don't express it very articulately? Do you remember my illustration about hotel guests who say, "I just want to feel at home"? Recall that I had to dig deeper to learn what that statement actually meant.

4. Start figuring out *how to meet those desires* as efficiently as possible. What systems will you need to create? How will you drive defects out of the operation? How will you serve customers' desires in a timely manner? And how will you and your team show a caring spirit? The combination of these things is what, over time, turns a satisfied customer into a loyal customer. They come to realize that every time they do business with you, it's a positive experience. They go away pleased. They think they'll probably come back next time and maybe spend even more. They trust you.

5. Think about how you're going to let the customer *individualize or customize the experience*, which is becoming a bigger deal every year in our economy. What if he or

she wants a chicken sandwich with *two* slices of tomato and only *half* a pickle and *very little* mustard? Are you going to force the person to accept the preordained condiments, or are you going to let personal preference rule? And how are you going to do that in a timely manner without causing chaos in the kitchen?

6. Meanwhile, how are you going to give your employees *a sense of belonging*, of buy-in, to the work? How are you going to inspire them rather than just order them around? Without this, your well-planned systems will be wide open to neglect, if not outright sabotage.

7. Plan how you're going to accurately measure what you've set out to accomplish. How will you know whether your customers are pleased? How will you know whether your employees are doing what the job requires? What yardsticks are you going to watch and keep watching?

8. Finally, a question for you personally: *Are you fully committed to making this happen?* Are you willing to take responsibility in the driver's seat? Will you stay focused, brushing away distractions? Will you rise above excuses and "explanations"? Leading means having a destination in mind, not just walking in a circle. To lead is to hold fervently to a vision of the future and then to guide the rest of the organization toward it.

One More Thing

All of the above, however, does not happen in a vacuum. Other leaders in your field are going through the same exercise, aiming to fulfill their own visions. You've got stiff competition, whether or not you want to think about it.

That leads me to make one further edit to the book title we talked about at the beginning of the chapter: **Do *with excellence* what the customer loves, and the money will follow.**

We have to distinguish ourselves from the rest, and the distinction is doing things a little better, a little more satisfying. *We do things with excellence.* The market segment is not critical here. A Mercedes needs to be excellent, but so does a Ford. If I'm running a simple shoe store, I want to create the kind of atmosphere that when someone comes in—even if they don't buy anything—they'll come back the next time they're looking to buy shoes.

When my colleagues and I started the Ritz-Carlton, we said, "We want to build the best hotel company in the world. Who are we up against? Who are the global leaders?" The three answers at that time were Hyatt, Hilton International (not domestic), and Intercontinental. How would we ever succeed?

We set out to do everything a little better than what those three were doing. We would be a little cleaner, a little friendlier, a little more knowledgeable every time we spoke to a guest about anything.

Actually, to be the *best* of anything is not the same as being *excellent*. You can be better than all your competitors and still have a gap to deal with when it comes to achieving *excellence*. What if a new competitor that outperforms you comes along? In the long run, excellence is what secures your future.

To quote a wise man from centuries past, "Whatever your hand finds to do, do it with all your might."[2] I saw this attitude in that first maître d' back in Germany when I was a teenager. He absolutely exuded excellence. It set the course for my working life.

WE HAVE TO
DISTINGUISH
OURSELVES
FROM THE REST

AND THE DISTINCTION IS
DOING THINGS A LITTLE *BETTER*
WE DO THINGS
WITH *EXCELLENCE*

I remember getting a letter from a businessman who, while driving back to the Denver airport after a conference in the Colorado mountains, had run into heavy traffic due to a worsening snowstorm. Traffic on the interstate had slowed to a crawl, and he realized he wasn't going to make his homeward flight—the last flight of the day.

He began calling hotels to see if he could get a room for the night. Of course, hundreds of other travelers had been doing the same thing, and the man couldn't find a reservation anywhere. What was he going to do—sleep on an airport bench overnight?

In desperation, he called the concierge of the Ritz-Carlton in Aspen, the ski resort more than two hundred miles back west in the mountains. "Can you help me?" he pleaded. "I'm going to be stuck overnight in Denver because of the snow." The interesting twist in this story is that the businessman hadn't even been staying at the Aspen Ritz-Carlton; his meeting had occurred at a different facility. But he thought that maybe, just maybe, this concierge would be willing to come to his aid.

"Certainly," said the man. "Let me see what I can do." Within minutes, he had performed some kind of magic and found the traveler a room for the night—not at a Ritz-Carlton, but at some other hotel near the airport.

In his grateful letter to me, the businessman wrote, "I just thought if anybody can give me the right service, it'll be the Ritz-Carlton. They'll help me." That is what you call going above and beyond—to the realm called "serving with excellence."

Daniel Webster (1782–1852) was perhaps the most powerful orator in American politics in the first half of the nineteenth century. He served in the House of Representatives and then in the US Senate, and he was secretary of state twice. Back when he was a young man, he said he thought he'd like to become a lawyer, but people had discouraged him. "We have so many lawyers already," they said. "The field is too crowded. You should choose something else."

Shaking his head no, he replied with this memorable sentence: "There is always room at the top."[3]

The drive to be the best, to be measurably better than the competition, is what brings personal fulfillment and also financial reward. When we set out to be excellent in our chosen category and refuse to settle for anything less, even as the years pile up and the economy goes into a skid, we will achieve our dreams. The common myths of business will have been exposed for what they are and replaced with reality. The vision will have come true.

THE REST OF
THE STORY

I am grateful for the opportunities I have had to pursue excellence in my field, training ladies and gentlemen to serve ladies and gentlemen. From my lowly start in a small German village, I have been privileged to travel the world and work with outstanding people.

But it all nearly came to a screeching halt back in 1992.

Ritz-Carlton was flying high. We had twenty-five hotels up and running, from Atlanta to Bali, with another fifteen on the drawing board for such exotic places as Hawaii and Shanghai. We had just won our first Malcolm Baldrige Award. The previous November, *Hotels* magazine had called me "corporate hotelier of the world."

I went in for my annual physical examination and was shocked to hear that I had a leiomyosarcoma of the colon, a rare malignancy that accounts for only 1 percent of cancer diagnoses. "We will operate to remove it," the surgeon said, "but it will come back within a year. It's like a snowstorm—it just shows up everywhere."

That evening, I looked at my dear wife, Sheri, and said, "This can't be happening!" Soon we were praying together, *God, please! Our children—they're only nine, five, and eighteen months—they won't even know me as they grow up. I won't be able to help them, to influence them.*

It didn't help that Sheri's father back in Pittsburgh was battling cancer at the same time. In fact, he passed away eighteen months later.

I made appointments to see more oncology specialists. Every one of them, after examining my case, confirmed the original opinion.

Soon I was screaming at God, trying to bargain with him. *I'll do anything you ask; just let me live for my family!* I found it hard even to say the Lord's Prayer, particularly the line "thy will be done." *Lord, please include my healing in your will,* I begged.

My high-flying career in the hotel world faded in importance. All the ambition, the strategic plans, the ego, the money, and the recognitions got stripped away. They weren't relevant anymore. When this kind of upheaval erupts in your life, it is easier to let God come and fill the vacuum. A Scripture from my boyhood confirmation class back in Germany returned to my mind: "He will cover you with his feathers, and under his wings you will find refuge; his faithfulness will be your shield and rampart."[1] I recited that verse again and again.

The Bible describes how when Jesus entered Jerusalem on Palm Sunday, his mild manner reminded people of a certain prophecy: "See, your king comes to you, gentle and riding on a donkey."[2] That is how it felt to me. God was quietly riding into the center of my panic.

I had been attending a weekly home-based Bible class with about thirty other men. Now, four of them said they wanted to come over and pray for me. This shocked my sense of reserve and privacy. (As the saying goes, "You can tell a German, but you can't tell him much!") But now in my desperate hour, I said okay.

Their prayers that evening seemed so deep, so heavy, so authentic. After they left, I said to myself, *I want to be a godly man like that.*

Fear Not

The surgery proceeded, and it was successful—for the time being. The next Monday, the technicians did a full body scan to see if some of the "snow" was already growing elsewhere. I was told to come back on Thursday to hear the results. *Why so long?* I wondered. I was tempted to launch into my spiel about customers needing *timeliness*, but I restrained myself.

On Wednesday night, Sheri and I were lying on the living room floor praying. I had never felt so close to her. We prayed that I could come back from all this. We prayed for our daughters; while the two younger ones didn't fully grasp what was going on, our nine-year-old was clearly aware that something was not good with Daddy.

We had been told that I would need to be checked every three months for new outbreaks of the sarcoma. We hoped against hope that these checkups wouldn't bring more bad news.

In the midst of our praying, a friend named John Watson knocked at the door. We invited him in. "Well," he said, "maybe I should tell you guys what happened to me before your operation. I woke up in the middle of the night, and I just knew somebody else was in the room. What happened next was that this 'somebody' said to me, 'Do not worry about your friend Horst. I have other plans for him. In fact, he will even do speaking for me—not only in English, but also in German.'"

Our anxiety subsided at that point. By the next day, I felt expectant as I returned to the doctor to hear the scan report. "You are totally cancer-free for now," he said. "Just come back in three months, and we'll see how things are going."

The Verdict of Time

As you know from reading this book, my body did not succumb to the cancer. My checkups continued to be clean. My work with Ritz-Carlton and later on with Capella resumed at a vigorous pace.

Though chemotherapy was recommended, I declined. Instead, I went on a macrobiotic diet for the next two years, seeking to hold steady.

The years kept passing, one after another. I did more speaking to business groups, university classes, and churches, not only here in America but back in my homeland as well. In November 2015, I was speaking at Johns Hopkins University in Baltimore. I found myself at an evening dinner with several oncologists. I happened to mention that I had survived cancer.

"What kind of cancer?" they wanted to know. I told them the name and a little about the case.

"Horst, you didn't have *that* cancer," one of the men flatly declared. "Otherwise, you wouldn't be sitting here. You would be long gone."

"Look," I protested, "I went to the best experts in the country. They all concurred."

"Well, that analysis twenty-some years ago was not as sophisticated as it is today," came the reply. "You didn't have that cancer—we can assure you." They asked where the treatment had been done.

"At Piedmont Hospital in Atlanta," I said.

"That's a good hospital," the one man answered. "They probably still have your slides. I'd like to see them."

So when I returned home, I called the CEO, whom I knew. He said he would check the archives. Sure enough, my file was brought up and sent to Baltimore.

Two weeks later, I got a call from the skeptical oncologist. "Next time you come this way, I want to meet you again," he said. "I've never met anybody who survived that cancer."

I can only say that God heard the desperate prayers of a man, his wife, and their friends. We had said to him, *Please be here!*—and he was.

I still meet with the study group that interceded for me, all these years later. In fact, I go to a second weekly group taught by a Bible scholar named Ken Boa. On Sundays, our family gains invaluable strength and insight from our worship at The Church of the Apostles. About four times a year, we open our home for an all-day seminar on some spiritual topic, welcoming up to fifty people at a time.

The foundation of God's truth lies at the center of my life in business. Whether I'm interacting with an employee, a customer, an investor, or even a competitor, I am aware that this person is one of the "others" Jesus had in mind when he gave the Golden Rule about treating them as I would want to be treated.[3]

When disputes arise over contract terms, with opposing lawyers battling back and forth, I hear the familiar words of the New Testament epistle, "Do not be anxious about anything, but in every situation, by prayer and petition, with thanksgiving, present your requests to God. And the peace of God, which transcends all understanding, will guard your hearts and your minds in Christ Jesus."[4] More than once I've seen the deadlock melt away as I have done my best and trusted God to handle the rest.

In retrospect, I think I was mostly a "Sunday Christian" until the onset of my cancer. This was a time when my business achievements lost all importance. They played no more role; they no longer sheltered me from my screaming need for hope. And hope at this point could only be found in Christ. So my decision for Christ (for hope) was a deep and permanent one. To tell the truth, I am today thankful for cancer—as well as grateful to have survived it.

And now you know the rest of my story.

NOTES

Chapter 1: Getting Inside Your Customer's Head

1. Michael Geheren, "Airline Goes 'Above and Beyond' to Help Mother Whose Son Went into Coma," *WGN*, May 27, 2015, http://wgntv.com/2015/05/27/airline-goes-above-and-beyond-to -help-mother-whose-son-went-into-coma.

Chapter 2: Customer Service Is *Everybody's* Job

1. To read Stephen Covey's telling of this incident, see his *The 7 Habits of Highly Effective People* (New York: Simon & Schuster, 1989), 140–42.

2. Kevin D. O'Gorman, "The Legacy of Monastic Hospitality," *Hospitality Review* 8, no. 3 (July 2006): 37, https://strathprints .strath.ac.uk/4975/6/strathprints004975.pdf.

3. O'Gorman, "The Legacy of Monastic Hospitality," 37.

4. See "Baldrige Performance Excellence Program," National Institute of Standards and Technology, www.nist.gov/baldrige/ about-baldrige-excellence-framework-education.

Chapter 5: Three Kinds of Customers (and Three Ways to Lose Them)

1. Wharton School of the University of Pennsylvania, "Wells Fargo: What Will It Take to Clean Up the Mess," *Knowledge@Wharton*, August 8, 2017, http://knowledge.wharton.upenn.edu/article/ wells-fargo-scandals-will-take-clean-mess.

2. "Forsake All Others: Mobile Technology Is Revamping Loyalty Schemes," *The Economist*, September 9, 2017, 64, www.econo mist.com/business/2017/09/07/mobile-technology-is-revamping -loyalty-schemes.

Chapter 6: More Than a Pair of Hands

1. Quoted in Bob Clinkert, "What Henry Ford Really Thinks of You," *Unleash the Masterpiece*, October 25, 2013, http://unleash themasterpiece.com/?p=543.
2. Henry Ford, *My Life and Work* (Garden City, NY: Doubleday, 1922), 72.
3. See Frederick Winslow Taylor, *The Principles of Scientific Management* (New York: Harper, 1911).
4. Leviticus 19:18 NIV.
5. Mark 12:31.
6. Jim Collins, "Good to Great," *Fast Company*, October 2001, www.jimcollins.com/article_topics/articles/good-to-great.html.

Chapter 7: First Things First

1. See Andrew Cave, "Culture Eats Strategy for Breakfast. So What's for Lunch?" *Forbes*, November 9, 2017, www.forbes.com/sites/ andrewcave/2017/11/09/culture-eats-strategy-for-breakfast-so -whats-for-lunch/#4e8774ae7e0f.

Chapter 8: Why Repetition Is a Good Thing

1. Covey, *The 7 Habits of Highly Effective People*, 152–54, 156.

Chapter 9: Managers Push; Leaders Inspire

1. James A. Autry, *Love and Profit: The Art of Caring Leadership* (New York: Morrow, 1992), 45, italics original. This book won the prestigious Johnson, Smith & Knisley Award for having the most impact on executive thinking in 1992.

2. Clayton M. Christensen, "How Will You Measure Your Life?" *Harvard Business Review,* July–August 2010, https://hbr.org/2010/07/how-will-you-measure-your-life.

3. Christensen, "How Will You Measure Your Life?"

4. Autry, *Love and Profit,* 17.

Chapter 10: Bridging the Gulf between Management and Labor

1. Aristotle, selections from *Nicomachean Ethics,* book 1, section 5, in *The Pocket Aristotle* (New York: Simon & Schuster, 1958), 165.

Chapter 11: Leading Is an Acquired Skill

1. William Shakespeare, *Twelfth Night,* act 2, scene 5, lines 1150–51, http://internetshakespeare.uvic.ca/doc/TN_M/scene/2.5/.

2. Quoted in *Google Answers,* "Are Leaders Born or Made?" April 24, 2005, http://answers.google.com/answers/threadview?id=513423.

3. Susan Cain, *Quiet: The Power of Introverts in a World That Can't Stop Talking* (New York: Crown, 2013), 53.

4. Chip Cutter, "The Inside Story of What It Took to Keep a Texas Store Chain Running in the Chaos of Hurricane Harvey," *LinkedIn,* September 2, 2017, www.linkedin.com/pulse/inside-story-what-took-keep-texas-grocery-chain-running-chip-cutter.

5. Quoted in Stuart Crainer and Des Dearlove, *What We Mean When We Talk about Innovation* (Oxford: Infinite Ideas, 2011), 13.

Chapter 13: A Leader's "Gut" Is Not Enough

1. "The Man with the Golden Gut: Programmer Fred Silverman Has Made ABC No. 1," *Time,* September 5, 1977, 46–49.

2. For more detail, see "Baldrige Excellence Framework," www.nist.gov/sites/default/files/documents/2016/12/13/2017-2018-baldrige-framework-bnp-free-sample.pdf; see also "About the Baldrige Excellence Framework," www.nist.gov/baldrige/about-baldrige-excellence-framework.

Chapter 14: Money and Love

1. Marsha Sinetar, *Do What You Love, the Money Will Follow: Discovering Your Right Livelihood* (New York: Dell, 1987).
2. Ecclesiastes 9:10 NIV.
3. Quoted in Martin Manser, *The Facts on File Dictionary of Proverbs* (New York: Infobase, 2002), 262.

Epilogue: The Rest of the Story

1. Psalm 91:4 NIV.
2. Matthew 21:5 NIV, quoting Zechariah 9:9.
3. Matthew 7:12; Luke 6:31.
4. Philippians 4:6–7 NIV.

ABOUT THE AUTHORS

From his humble beginnings in a German village, **Horst Schulze** has risen to become a world-recognized pacesetter in the hospitality industry. He came to the United States in 1964, working in Hilton hotels, then spent nine years with the Hyatt Corporation, where he rose from a local manager to regional vice president and then corporate vice president.

In 1983, he was recruited to help shape a new brand for North America: the Ritz-Carlton. Over the next nineteen years, the company grew under his leadership from zero luxury hotels to fifty-five across eleven countries. As president and COO, he was repeatedly honored with various awards—"corporate hotelier of the world," said *Hotels* magazine in 1991. Three years later, he won ASQ's Ishikawa Medal for having "a major positive impact on the human aspects of quality."

The pinnacle of the Ritz-Carlton years was winning the United States government's prestigious Malcolm Baldrige National Quality Award—not once, but twice (1992, 1999).

Schulze then raised the bar even higher in 2002 by striking out on his own to start the ultraluxury Capella Hotel Group, with top-of-the-line facilities as far-flung as Singapore, Düsseldorf, Shanghai, the Caribbean, Bali, and New Zealand.

Along the way, he has been in high demand as a speaker at business leadership gatherings, university assemblies, CEO groups, the Willow Creek Global Leadership Summit simulcast, and individual companies that request his consultation. In this work he is represented by the Washington Speakers Bureau.

Schulze and his wife, Sheri, are the parents of four grown daughters and live in Atlanta.

Dean Merrill is responsible for nine of his own books, plus another forty collaborative titles, some of which have achieved national bestseller status and won publishing industry awards. In the business field, he helped create *More Than a Hobby* by David Green, founder and CEO of the Hobby Lobby retail chain—a book that is still in print more than a decade after its 2005 release. Merrill and his wife, Grace, live in Colorado Springs.

Interested in tools and resources
to apply the principles of this book at scale
across your organization or team?
Explore www.needtolead.com